The One-Week Budget

Get One Step Closer to Financial Freedom by Creating an Easy Money Management System That Will Help You Make More Money and Keep You Debt Free

Complete Volume

By

Income Mastery

The One-Week Budget

Get One Step Closer to Financial Freedom by
Creating an Easy Money Management System
That Will Help You Make More Money and
Keep You Debt Free

Volume 1

The One-Week Budget

Get One Step Closer to Financial Freedom by
Creating an Easy Money Management System
That Will Help You Make More Money and
Keep You Debt Free

Volume 2

The One-Week Budget

Get One Step Closer to Financial Freedom by
Creating an Easy Money Management System
That Will Help You Make More Money and
Keep You Debt Free

Volume 3

The following book is written with the goal of providing information as accurate and reliable as possible. In any case, the purchase of this book considers that both the publisher and the author are not experts in the topics covered and that the recommendations or suggestions made here are for entertainment purposes only. Professionals should be consulted as necessary before undertaking any of the actions mentioned here.

This statement is considered fair and valid by both the American Bar Association and the Committee of the Publishers Association and is considered legal throughout the United States.

In addition, the transmission, duplication or reproduction of any of the following works, including specific information, shall be considered an illegal act regardless of whether it is in electronic or printed form. This extends to the creation of a secondary or tertiary copy of the work or a recorded copy and is only permitted with the express written consent of the author. All additional rights reserved.

The information on the following pages is generally considered to be a truthful and accurate description of the facts and, as such, any lack of attention, use or misuse of the information in question by the reader will cause the resulting actions to be solely within his or her

Table of Contents

The One-Week Budget: Volume 1

Get One Step Closer to Financial Freedom by Creating an Easy Money Management System That Will Help You Make More Money and Keep You Debt Free

By

Income Mastery

Introduction

We have all struggled to achieve our long-term goals. I'm sure you know people who are highly successful, and you don't know how they got there. You can see co-workers taking trips to tourist destinations that are simply not within your economic reach. Or people who are buying cars, apartments and you don't see them worried. And on the other hand, there are endless people who have these things but when you talk to them you can feel the level of stress they have because they are up to their necks in debt. But then you see people who have what they need, live comfortably and have nothing to worry about. Do you know who these people are? Those who have achieved financial freedom. Haven't you wondered how they did it? The answer is simple, good money management is not magic, it is organization and discipline.

The vast majority of truly successful people are those who have achieved financial freedom. And what does that mean? Summarized in the most concrete and quickest way, financial freedom is the ability to live without worrying about money at any time. Some even try to define it in a more economical way for our society, as the number of months you could live if you stopped working right now. But beyond that, it is the simple, but immensely important, the feeling of living without a single concern related to money.

Financial freedom is linked to a well-being individual's economic. But beware, it has nothing to do with wealth. You can earn modestly and still have financial freedom. Why? Because financial freedom doesn't mean you have enough money to buy everything you want, no matter what the price. True financial freedom has minimalism as one of its greatest and most important pillars. In learning to live with what is right and with what is necessary. So, the combination of minimalism and financial freedom can allow us to enjoy life without having to worry about money. So, to have financial freedom, you don't need to have high incomes. It's about training your mind.

In this section, you'll find a number of methods, tips and rules that will help you better control your budget and spending habits so you can get closer to the financial freedom we all crave. We're going to start with a budget you can put together in seven days. Let's start with the simplest knowledge and exercises you can do to get you started on this road to financial freedom and let's get to see methods like the CLARK method, which is a more advanced way to organize your expenses and limit them so you have more control over your budget.

Just remember that you can modify all this to suit you and to go sideways with your life habits. It is important that you work with yourself in order to achieve something of much greater impact.

Day One

The first day of this process are small exercises that you can practice in order to improve your understanding of your monthly expenses at the most basic level. They may be simple, but they are still highly effective.

Step 1: Write down and organize your monthly expenses

This step is self-explanatory. You can't underestimate how important it is to write and organize monthly expenses. For example, you can consume whatever you want, whenever you want. Like, for example, a nice meal at night. Suddenly you check your account statement on the phone and think, "Look, I still have x amount of money left. I can pay for that dessert I've been wanting to buy for a long time!". Let's be honest, you can do it if you want, but it's going to cause you problems if you're not organizing your expenses correctly and spending your money impulsively.

Memory can betray you. What if this month you had to pay one of your fees for a trip you took on vacation? What if this month you borrowed money from a co-worker, and he asks you back? What if this month is your partner's birthday or anniversary? And it doesn't necessarily mean you've forgotten, but your memory might not realize the extra expenses of next month. That's why writing down your expenses at the beginning of each month is one of the most sensible things you can do. It's what makes the difference between a money guru and the rest of the people.

Make a list and write down everything you know for the next month. Do you have to shop this month? Write them down and figure out what the total will be. Do you have a doctor's appointment? Write it down and add it up. A good organized list doesn't have to be complex. An efficient list could look like this:

Next month:

- **Shopping Cart: 80**

- **Medical appointment: 150**

- **Anniversary Date: 100**

- **Total: 330**

With a list like this, no matter how simple it may be, you have to reserve a total of 330 of your income for that month so that you don't have financial problems and/or worries.

Later you will see how to better segment a much more complex and organized list of monthly expenses. But being able to organize yourself to write down your expenses works even easier. It is not necessary to create documents with tables in Microsoft Excel or within Google Drive. The important thing is to keep track of expenses so that you can easily recognize them and help yourself control and own your finances.

Don't forget that all these are recommendations, if you feel that it does not seem to work, don't worry, keep trying and eventually you will find a formula that goes perfectly with you and your lifestyle. And don't feel bad if you don't have the time to organize yourself like this book is going to recommend later. Basic lists, such as the one in the example above, will always be useful. In conclusion, as long as the list you've made helps you to remember and set aside your expenses, the list works.

Step 2: Recognize the limits of your money - How Much You Earn and How Much You Spend

In this step you must recognize the limits of your own income. One of the most important things we've already seen is having your next expenses in the sights, noted and listed, so that your memory doesn't fail you and you end up with financial worries; if you're reading this, you're not looking for worries, you're looking for financial peace of mind.

This step invites you to compare, the way you decide (it can be a simple handmade table, a document in notes or a Microsoft Excel table) how much you earn and how much you spend. If in the previous step you made your list of upcoming expenses, it's time to compare it against your income. For example, if your salary was 1,000, and we continue to use the expenses from the previous example, your chart should look something like this:

Profit	Expenses
Salary: 1000	Month: 330

Why is this board important? Because it will help you organize, know and understand everything about the money you can spend so that you are free of all guilt and all worry, in those tastes or cravings that may arise simply on occasions of everyday life. Right now, you can see that in the example the individual has 670 left to use in whatever he wants for the rest of the month. However, later on, we'll see a better way to use this money to bring you closer to financial freedom. Did you crave your favorite dessert from your favorite store, but don't know how it affects your finances? Don't worry, you'll be able to buy it eventually without feeling that worry.

These steps will help you reach that much sought-after freedom where you will be truly free of financial worries. We'll see recommendations on how to use the information in this step later.

Step 3: Start saving your money in the bank.

One of the best things you can do is save your money in the bank. A lot of banks give interest to keep your money there. No matter how small the amount of bank interest, it's worth it. You can save your money on your own, but having it in the bank gives you information, security and a minimum profit. And that's why financial institutions can become your best allies to help transform your financial freedom plans into reality.

Let's tell you some of the advantages that banks give you to save before keeping your money "under the mattress" like in the old days. Banks offer you the possibility to increase your savings with their different interest rates. This means that just by keeping your savings in a bank account you're already generating income, even if it's minimal. Banks also give you security, which is much more prudent than carrying or storing cash; which is much easier to steal. Banks also offer you the possibility to access offers depending on the type of account you have or the type of card. For example, some cards accumulate miles so you can travel to different destinations, and many services offer discounts for online payments.

Banks also give you speed when it comes to financial transactions. When you have your money in an account, you can pay for various services and make transfers through the different customer service channels offered by financial institutions. Today, there is no longer a need to queue up to make payments, which can also carry security risks if you are carrying the money to pay cash. The different services give you speed and security like never before.

It should be noted that there are other options apart from banks. If you only want an account where you can save and where you don't plan to withdraw money immediately, some financial institutions offer you the option to have and register an account that gives you the best interests but you can't withdraw your money more than once a year; but you can deposit in that account without limit, it's an account to make your savings grow. That's optimal for an account where you're just looking to save your money and get the best financial results. Remember, "It's not how much money you make, it's how much money you keep."

Other accounts are the classic ones that generate less interest than the one mentioned above but that will allow you to withdraw up to a large limit per day from ATMs and an even larger limit from bank windows.

But most importantly, it is the access to your account information that all modern banks provide you through various means. Chances are that your bank has a cell phone application where you can see the movements of your money, you will be able to see how much of your money has been spent and in what; in addition to seeing the date that the organization will facilitate you.

It is important to be clear about the benefits each bank can give you. Ignorance is the greatest friend of poverty. Information is free and you should use a portion of your time to go to the bank to have all of your questions answered.

Day Two

On this day it is up to us to better sort out our expenses and identify them as what they are. Are they things we can get rid of or are they necessary for our lives? Having this answer means doing something more difficult, sacrificing those tastes that do not add (and rather subtract) to the possibility of achieving your financial goals. This day teaches steps to identify our tastes and limit them, so they don't get out of control.

Step 4: Segment Your Spend into Fixed and Variable

In this step we are going to look at one of the bases of finance at both the company and personal level. Separate, identify and organize your variable and adjustable fixed expenses. We'll start with the Fixed Expenses. In the example I showed you in Step 1, where you had to make a simple list to record and organize your monthly expenses, all expenses were variable. I'll explain why next.

What expenses fall into the category of fixed expenses? Those who are always the same and are not going to change even as the months go by. The most common fixed costs are, for example, rental costs, house services

(Internet, telephone and cable), insurance that you pay (medical, car, accident, etc.), your memberships to services (such as gym, Netflix, Spotify, etc.). Having these expenses as clearly as possible is one of the most important steps that will lead you to the financial freedom you want.

What expenses fall under the variable expenses category? All those that vary in price from month to month. For example: water and light. These costs vary according to how much you have consumed and are not always the same. You can also shop at home, when you go to the supermarket or market to buy food. The complicated thing about variable expenses is that you can be out of your control like the price of gasoline or the dollar in the market. But you can also limit and organize your own expenses, which we'll see in step 7 below.

By properly organizing these expenses, we can identify what the major expenses are. Giovanna Prialé, president of the AFP Association says: "What is urgent and important in our budget is that which we cannot live without even a month. For example: services, because if we don't pay, they can cut off our electricity. However, if you have a craving or want to celebrate with a bottle of wine you must understand that, while it may be your need, it is just a desire.

In this step, it is a question of correctly defining fixed costs as costs that we cannot do without and variables as those that we have to control in the best way. The next step will teach you a couple of effective tips to reduce your expenses.

Step 5: Reduce your expenses

This step asks you to prioritize your expenses and identify all those you can reduce to obtain a better amount of savings. Saving is not magic; it is a voluntary organization where you consciously seek to increase the amount of money you have available by reducing the expenses you don't need. And there's the key word, need.

While we mentioned earlier that you can give yourself a couple of tastes, the key to getting closer and closer to financial freedom is to limit them. You have to clearly separate what is taste from what is need. For example: water, electricity, food, transport and health are necessities. Technology, sweets, accessories, liquors and ornaments are tastes.

To maintain exceptional finances, you don't have to spend more than you need. Giovanna Prialé, president of the AAFP (Association of AFPs) in Peru, comments that the basis for understanding personal finances is **sacrificing some desires in order to fulfill your objectives**. The most recommended thing is that you reserve a percentage of your budget equivalent to ten percent (10%) and destine it to savings. And to find a motivation, it's good to set a goal, such as going on a holiday and visiting another country. With a clear objective, the effort will be maintained.

Having previously seen what fixed expenses and variable expenses are, you can understand that fixed expenses are the expenses that have to be prioritized; the expenses where you put your needs. While some debts can be variable amounts, you have to treat them with the same urgency and importance as a fixed expense. It is important that in order to pay your debts, if you have any, you derive at least thirty percent (30%) of your total budget. Ideally, don't get into debt, but if you have to get into debt, always try to keep them below 30% to avoid financial problems.

Unforeseen expenses such as going to a concert or repairing broken ones are expenses you can't anticipate. If you are using the numbers from the examples above, what you have left would be what you can use for variable expenses. You then have to add the cost of your fixed expenses, ten percent for savings (10%) and thirty percent to pay any debts or commitments you may have (30%). The total number of the sum you subtract from your budget and what remains you can freely spend on variable expenses.

Let's make a quick example. If your budget is 1,000, that means that thirty percent would be approximately 300 and ten percent would be 100. Those 100 go to savings, those 300 go to pay off debts. These percentages rise to a total of 400. Subtracting it from your budget would leave you with 600. Let's say the total of your fixed costs is 350, if you subtract them from your remaining budget (600), you would keep about 250. These 250 can be spent freely on variable costs without the need to feel any guilt.

Remember, these are all recommendations, but the point is still that you must spend much less than your budget. If you're spending more than your monthly budget, you won't be able to get financial freedom.

Day Three

Step 6: Adding to Your Savings

In this step it's time to see how to increase your savings. We saw in the previous step that in order to reduce your expenses it is good to allocate ten percent of your budget to savings. Now let's see how you can better define your savings so you can add money while you're motivated.

One of the most important things is to define your savings goals. Choose goals for your savings, such as buying a bicycle, a notebook or going on vacation to a nearby place. Maybe it can be something that truly brings you closer to financial freedom, something like saving to start a business. You will have to see what is most important to you and your future, you will have to set goals. And when we talk about goals, it's important to be able to classify them clearly. We have 3 types of clear goals: short term, medium term and long term.

Short-term goals are goals that should take no more than 2 years to reach. These are things like buying a bicycle, buying a laptop or notebook, and/or going on vacation somewhere nearby. Medium-term goals are goals that should not take more than 7 years to reach. They are things like collecting the money needed for the down payment of an apartment, buying a motorcycle or a car, and/or going on vacation to another continent with full payment. Long-term goals are goals that can take several years to achieve. These goals are important life goals. Such as saving for a better retirement. With clear goals, achieving your life goals is more than possible.

While there are times when, after drawing up your accounts, you feel that you do not have enough to save, it is preferable to save even a smaller amount. Don't make the mistake of thinking "I'm going to save once...". That's one of the worst things you can do, because as time goes by, new expenses come up that you didn't expect. The best time to save is now. It doesn't matter how much you save; it matters that you're saving. Remember that even though that money may feel very small, if you have it in some financial institution, you can generate interest.

Step 7: Redefine your monthly expenses

In this step we will redefine your monthly expenses. We're going to give you some tips so you can get organized, so you know when to spend money and when not to.

There is a rule called the "30 Day Rule". This is the easiest practice to implement, but at the same time, one of the most difficult to follow. It's about this: simply wait 30 days before you buy items you know are not in basic need and resist the temptation to buy them when they first come to your mind. Why is this rule so effective? Because after a month, you'll be able to tell if you're really interested in that product or if it was just an impulse. If you keep thinking about the product, you can buy it, if you have forgotten about it, then it was just an impulse and that impulse will have calmed down.

Another rule is that you keep the change you get on the street. Normally, walking around with cash makes it much more common to fall into the temptation of petty cravings, precisely because the price is lower. What this rule recommends is that you get a piggy bank or something similar that prevents you from taking that money out until the container is full. Then, the change you get on the street can be saved for an unexpected event, so it does not affect your budget. Before you know it, you could have saved enough to pay for your fixed costs of that package. Don't underestimate the "piggy of savings".

A very useful thing is to limit your budget to variable expenses. Basically, it's putting yourself on a spending cap. For example, in debt, we talked about keeping it below thirty percent (30%). Banks usually recommend that a person not get into debt for more than 60%-70% of their monthly income. But keeping your debts as low as possible is the best way to save. So, you might as well limit your debt cap on variable expenses. Let's just say you have about 300 of your salary left over. Earlier we said that you can use what over freely, but it is much better also to put a limit on variable expenses. In this case, if you have 300 left, you could set your limit of variable expenses to 200. That way, you always have 100 left for any eventuality. And if there isn't, you'll have those 100 next month, and if you use the same variable spending limit again, they'll turn into 200.

Another rule is never go shopping without being perfectly clear about what you need. If you haven't planned a shopping list, the chance that you'll buy something on impulse that you don't really need is much greater. However, sometimes a list is not enough, and you don't remember everything you need until you see it. In that case, there are a couple of tips. One of them is to check the expiration date. Some food products can be very close to the day of purchase and if you are thinking of using it for a while is better to buy freshly labeled products. Another tip is to take advantage of the day's discounts. Always check the catalog or discount magazine because they usually include many basic consumer products. Another tip is to go to the nearest place to your home. This with the goal that you can walk, which will force you to buy what is fair and necessary not to go with too much burden, something that does good to your health and your budget. And these are just some of the rabbits that are worth following if you go shopping without being prepared.

Here are some things you can do to redefine your monthly expenses. Remember, it's all about clarity, knowing what you need and controlling your impulses. All of this will help you redefine your monthly expenses in the best possible way.

Step 8: Plan Your Dollars

The name of this step "Plan your Dollars" alludes to some of the typical plans of countries like the United States to create a plan that allows you to have a good management of expenses.

Making a budget plan is basically organizing a plan for every "dollar" you have. It is not magic or anything like that, but it can bring you much closer to financial freedom and live with much less stress.

One of the most popular and useful plans in American culture is the 50%, 30%, and 20% strategy. In this budget plan, fifty percent of your budget goes to your needs, no more than thirty percent goes to tastes and at least twenty percent has to go to pay off debts and save. This means that if your budget is 1000, you can derive 500 for your needs, 300 for your tastes and 200 to pay debts and save. This is a very simple plan in case you find it too complicated to follow what we have written above.

But apart from this, we will later implement a plan known as the CLARK method. Developed by money expert Clark Howard. In the following steps you will see how to start it following each of the letters of the CLARK method.

Day Four

This day you take advantage of to write down your goals and start putting budgets together. Find out everything you need to find out so that the next day you can use all your knowledge to start recording your data and continue your plan. Today you're starting to put your own plan into action.

Step 9: Time to implement your own plan

This step is one of the shortest. This step invites you to implement your own plan and make your own budget with the above information. Take the day to be able to write down, schedule and put all the information we have discussed up to this point. Take advantage of the day to go to the banks you are interested in and ask about their interest rates, account types, etc. If you have a job, try asking for permission and say you have to go to the bank to organize your finances.

Also, take advantage of the day so that you can write your monthly budget, so that you can write down your fixed and variable costs, so that you can segment your budget in the different percentages, so that you can plan how much you are going to save and so that you can write down your short, medium and long term goals.

Once you have everything ready, you will use the next day to make your CLARK budget. In order to do this, it is important that you have all the necessary information at hand.

Day Five

On this day, you are going to aim at your favorite list and number management software, one of the most effective methods for budget control. You can do it in the program you prefer or do it by hand.

Step 10: Creating a grid for your budget

Today, there are many software's that can solve and help us with both trivial and important tasks. For finance, there are a number of programs ready to help us with all our goals and economic data. Among this great variety of programs, one of the most used for lists and data all over the world is Microsoft Excel, which we recommend using for this step. If you do not have Microsoft Office programs there are alternatives such as Google Drive programs, specifically referring to the very good alternative Google Sheets. There are also Open Office programs, a free version that was released as a free alternative to Microsoft Office.

The first thing you need to create a budget grid in one of these programs is the information you are going to write down. You should already have a very clear idea of the information we are going to use if you have carefully followed the previous steps of the previous days.

Gridding your personal budget is one of the most important steps in moving closer to financial freedom. It's also one of the most important steps in keeping your buying and spending habits under control and building a solid financial foundation for you and your family. A grid also helps you prioritize expenses, keep a record that tells you exactly what you've spent on, helps you pay off your debts, put long-term plans in place and be able to carry them out until they're fully completed.

Making a basic budget is something that doesn't require much science. As we mentioned before, you can use a program like Microsoft Excel, Google Sheets or the Open Office grid program, but you can also make your grid physically using nothing more and nothing less than paper, pencil or pencil and a ruler. The steps are the same no matter what you do your grid. It is recommended that you have the following in your grid for your personal budget:

-   A list of your income.

-   A list of your expenses.

-   Calculate your Net Income (after taxes).

-   Adjust your expenses.

-   Track your expenses.

On the list for your income, you should write down the total income you bring home each month. Focus on what you know to be reliable, what you will or will not bring home. So, don't include irregular income such as overtime or freelance work for a couple of hours. When you earn extra income, you should focus on paying off debts or saving them if you don't have debts. And if you work as a freelancer or are starting a business, and your income does not have an exact amount, then make an estimate of how much is your average monthly income and subtract from that estimate ten percent (10%), so that even if you are below your average you are not short of income. This information goes in the first column of your grid and you can name it "Income" as the title of the column.

In the list of your expenses, which you should already have clearer based on the previous steps, you write down all your types of expenses. Start with fixed expenses like your debts, rent or mortgage, internet, cable, Netflix and more. Make a list for the expenses, write the names and next to it another list to put, on the right side of the names, the price of the expenses. After that, give your last ballots or bills a check of what you have to pay to the banks or credit card. Use real numbers without omitting anything, do not omit or cents that can add up to some important number. Group common expenses, as if you went to McDonalds twice, write down only once and add up the result of the two times you went. Add up the value of all of them and you'll have your real expenses for the month.

The moment of truth comes. It's time to calculate your net income, which is basically how much money is left in your budget from your monthly income, once you've subtracted the total from your monthly expenses. Ideally, the resulting number should be positive. If it's not, it means that, on a monthly average, you're accumulating debt, and that's not good for you.

Then it's your turn to adjust your expenses. Just review the list of monthly expenses you've written on your grid and ask yourself what expenses you can actually reduce; and if you can eliminate even better. For example, let's say you usually spend about $750 at the grocery store doing house shopping and spend an average of about $250 going out to eat. So maybe you can be more careful what you spend on food, save a little and try to only spend $600 on grocery shopping and only $200 on eating out. That saves you about $150 from grocery shopping and about $50 from eating out expenses, a total of $200 in savings. Also look at your fixed costs and see if there are any that you can modify.

Finally, it's your turn to track your spending for next month. Focus on those categories where you decided to make changes and those that are related to your behavior and spending habits, such as home shopping, eating out, entertainment expenses (movies, concerts, parties, etc.) and what you spend on your hobby (Video games, sports, etc.) Keep track of everything you spend on those categories and try to keep your expenses always below your next month's goal. And if they are below the previous month analyze why to see how you can always keep expenses down.

You have to spend less than you earn and save the surplus to increase your emergency savings funds or some short-term, medium-term or long-term goal. Now, in the next step we'll see how to use a slightly more complex grid and we'll look at it in more detail. We will use the CLARK method.

Day Six

Take this day to organize your CLARK grid, one of the best ways to organize, track and clear your budget. We'll look at it in detail during the next step and it will help you get closer and closer to financial freedom.

Step 11: Segment your grid using the CLARK method.

In the previous step we saw how to use simple grids to get started. Now let's start segmenting our grid using one of the best known and most effective methods to make your own knowledge grid. This is known as **CLARK** for its figures: Calculate your income, list your expenses, analyze your spending and set goals, Record everything, and Knock out debt and build your savings.

CLARK's first step, which would become C, is about calculating your income. If you have followed the above steps to the letter, then you should have no problem filling this out. First, you have to record and calculate how much income you are bringing home per month. This includes your salary, after calculating what you subtract from taxes and deductions, and any additional income you have.

CLARK's next step, which would become the L, is about writing down a list of all your expenses. Again, if you've followed the steps above, you should be much clearer about how to do this CLARK step we're in; you've already written down your expenses in the steps above. First, make a list of your last month's expenses (to maintain good finances it is recommended to keep ballots and bills for each month) and start by writing them separately in different categories, which will be your budget categories: like your mortgage or rent, house purchases, cell phone bill, internet, etc. It's also good to categorize, for your monthly budget, annual or semi-annual expenses so that they don't surprise you and you're ready when it's time to pay for them. For example, if you pay about 600 car insurance every 6 months, you could set aside about 100 each month and keep them in your savings account for your next payment. You can consider organizing and scheduling automatic payments or transfers from your bank account for these types of payments that are not as regular but always arrive.

CLARK's next step, which would become A, is to analyze your expenses and set goals. We have already seen different types of goals and there is no problem with using the goals we saw in the previous steps. However, CLARK's goals are set in such a way that they are monthly (as opposed to what we saw in the previous steps as short term, medium term and long-term goals) and also necessary for this method of work. In this step, you have to budget realistically, monthly goals for each of the categories you have made. In the grid you are building inside one of the specialized programs (like Microsoft Excel or Google Sheets inside Google Drive), you will do the following: In the first column you put "Budget Categories" and underneath you list your expenses, like for example, mortgage or rent, home purchases, telephone, internet, etc. In the second column you put "Planned" where you will write down how much you should spend per month, which is what you already have listed. In the third column, you put "Paid" which is what you actually paid at the end of the month as opposed to what you had "planned" to pay. In the fourth column you put "Need Help" and leave the list below the title blank. In the fifth column put "Looks good" and leave the list blank below the title as in the fourth column. What will you do with this information and how will you use this table?:

- Plan your expenses by limiting a maximum of "dollars" (or your country's currency) for each category you have made.

- You will need to highlight or mark "Needs Help" in the fourth column for the categories you want to focus on the most.

- You will need to record how much you have actually spent in the "Paid" column,

- If you are satisfied with the expenses in any of your categories, you can highlight or mark the category in the "Looks Good" column.

When it comes to budgeting, CLARK suggests an approach to behavioral changes in the budget and not just numbers can help you stay on top of it. Some of his ideas are the following:

- Invest 10% of every dollar you earn into a retirement fund.

- If you have credit card debt, CLARK recommends that you freeze (literally, so you can't use it) your credit card and budget only with cash.

- Focus on preparing your own meals and bring your own food to work instead of eating out. The savings are greater.

CLARK's next step, which would become the R, is to record your expenses throughout the month. The only way to keep yourself responsible for your expenses is to record them as the month passes. There are many ways to record your transactions, you can use the Google Drive program like Google Sheets that we saw in the previous example, or you can use budget applications like Mint and YNAB (You Need A Budget). Reviewing and evaluating your spending habits at least once a week for the purpose of finding patterns and making necessary adjustments to your budget is one of the things that will bring you closer and closer to financial freedom.

CLARK's next step, which would become the K, is to eliminate debt and build your savings. Finally, in this

CLARK step, you use the money you have left over from your budget to reach your Long-Term goals faster. Prioritize things like paying off your credit card debts and building and/or saving into an emergency fund. Remember, "Once you're living on less than you earn, there are no absolutely bad decisions. But there are some that are better than others. You create freedom and your own choices when you're simply living on less than you earn." Money expert Clark Howard points out.

Day Seven

On the last day, we're going to look at the little tips so you can get closer and closer to financial freedom.

Step 12: Pay your bills in advance.

Paying your bills and debts in advance is one of the most important things you should do to avoid falling into financial problems that become constant worries. There's no worse concern than money. So, paying your bills in advance will help you live with less stress and bring you closer to financial freedom.

Now, it's important to be able to control your bill payment so they don't get out of control and it's not always easy to do so. That's why we're now going to give you some tips you can use to train yourself or help yourself pay your bills in advance. Here are some tips you can use to your advantage:

- Sign up for automatic payments. While many subscription services automatically charge you at the end of the month, you need to schedule this for truly important payments such as your rent. This gives you the option to have the amount you must pay automatically withdrawn from your bank account and paid as soon as your invoices are available.

- Use financial programs with automatic bill reminders: Both Microsoft Money and Quicken have features that can alert you days or weeks before your bill arrives, or you have to pay it. This is incredibly useful if you don't usually have a lot of time to program yourself. You do it once and it always warns you.

- Consolidate your bills where you can: Let's say you pay internet, cable and telephone from the same company. Instead of paying 3 different invoices, you could try contacting the company to see if they can charge you in one invoice. This way you are less likely to miss your payment date.

- Organize your invoices: You should have your invoices organized by due date. Make it a habit to check the due date of each invoice and write it down somewhere, better if it's on your phone's calendar as a reminder. This will help you to organize them better, since you will have an immediate and visual reminder about what bill you have to pay now. Extra advice? Always write it down one day before the due date. So, you have time to be prepared for any eventuality.

- Give your payment time to reach the recipient: You have to contact the institution or individual you are going to pay so that you know how many days it takes the system they use to process payments. This is even more important if you are trying to pay your bills on weekends or holidays, as the vast majority of banks do not make paperwork during those days. If you don't want the deadline to beat you, always pay in advance.

- Learn your billing cycle: Analyze and review invoices from previous months and make a list of the order in which they normally appear. You will notice that they have something in common and that they fall into one of two categories. Some are shipped the first days of the month (such as 5) and others are shipped on the last days of the month (such as 25). As soon as you get your bills, pay the ones that are due before your next paycheck. If you don't have enough money in your bank account to regularly pay your bills before your next paycheck, contact your creditors to see if they can help you by moving your payment dates. They can usually help you with these changes. Just report to the bank and make the necessary arrangements with the right person. There are always bank staff ready to answer your questions.

More tips to reduce your expenses

By this point you must have finished these 7 days of budget. Now, all the points mentioned are going to help you, but you must see how implement they are to the routine of your own life. If you don't think you have the discipline to follow them, no problem. You don't have to do everything. It's enough that you do some of the things to get started and then you can go back to this reading to see the most complex methods and writings.

So, now we'll give you tips that you can apply freely without having to follow any rules. Here are a few valuable tips on how to reduce your expenses so you can save and manage your budget the best way. Because the biggest problem that keeps you from getting closer and closer to the financial freedom, you're looking for is not that you earn too little money, it's that you spend too much and don't allow yourself to save. That's why the following tips are designed to help you regulate your buying impulses:

- Keep track of every expense at hand: We've seen it through the previous steps, but you should continue to record your expenses as notes on your cell phone or in some small booklet you carry in your pocket. This will make you never forget absolutely nothing you have spent your important money on. This is separate from the budgets in the previous steps. It's very easy to forget what the money was spent on, writing down every expense you make during the day will help you to have more control over your budget. In addition, you can check what you spend on and when you see that it turns out to be a considerably large number, you will think twice before continuing to spend more.

- Have a travel limit: Normally, when we go on a trip, it is common to go with a travel bag. That's the money we're going to use during the trip. However, we tend to carry more than we really need. You need to limit the expenses on a trip, really put how much you're going to spend separate from how much you're going to carry. If you can make a budget especially dedicated to that time you are going to be traveling, even better.

- Have your budget at hand: Just as we assemble grids, it's important that you have the relevant information at hand. That you can access it when you are on the street to remind you always and never accidentally exceed the amount. And this becomes more important, and may even become absolutely necessary, if you have several categories of budgets as we put together in some of the examples. You have to have at hand how much is your limit of each expenditure you make.

- Consider only using cash: Remember that the budget you put together will be of no use to you if you can't follow it to the letter. Using cash has very good benefits. First, studies say you spend less on cash than on credit or debit cards, because you can clearly see and feel how you spend the money. Second, if you don't use credit, then there is no horrible possibility that you will spend more than you earn ending up in debt. And third, if you already have your departures budgeted, then you only carry with you an amount of cash equal to the spending limit of your departures. That way, you'll always be below what you have to spend, and you won't go over the limit.

- Try using a system of envelopes: In the previous tip we saw to use cash. The envelope system is an evolution on the subject of cash. This is about taking cash for the various types of budget ceiling of each category and putting the exact amount of the ceiling inside the envelope. For example, you have an envelope for your home shopping and an envelope for eating out. So, when an envelope is empty, you don't spend in that category until next month when you fill it up again.

- Freeze your credit cards: If you really want to control how much you spend, avoiding credit cards is one of the most important things you can do. And if you don't have much self-control to do so, freezing your credit card is one of the best things you can do to help. However, you may not want to get rid of your credit cards because it's always good to develop a credit history by making payments when you owe, and you behave responsibly towards yourself.

- Use the 24-hour shopping rule: If you want to realize when something is an impulse and you're not spending your money rampantly without realizing the consequences, take some time to think about shopping. While we saw the 30-day rule, this rule is different because it does not apply to the product but to the price. For example, you say your 24-hour limit is tied to $50. That means that if something costs $50 or more, you have to think about it and give it to yourself 24 hours before you buy it. This rule also tells you to add hours according to $50 intervals. What does that mean? That if something costs $150, then you should think about it and give it to yourself about 72 hours before buying it, since $150 dollars is 3 times the limit value of your 24-hour rule. In the same way that if something costs $100, then you give yourself two days (48 hours) to think about it before buying it.

- Put days of 0 expenses: Another one of the best ways to reduce your expenses is to simply decide not to buy anything. Since you obviously still have to spend on necessary things like food, water and electricity, this method consists of choosing one day of the month not to spend. Even better if you do it a week. For example, every 17th of every month or every Wednesday of every week you will not spend any budget at all. When you schedule one of these days, you have to commit not to buy. There is also the 0

Expense Month where you only shop and spend on what you need; but no eating out, cravings, spending on your hobby, etc. In addition, one of the indirect benefits is that you train your mind to discipline itself to spend less.

- Create a savings game: If you're a person who has a hard time setting a limit and putting together a budget because you find it tedious or boring, there are a couple of ways to transform your savings into small, entertaining game rules to help you follow them. For example:

  - Every $5 bill you get for change when you pay with cash, you must keep it in a special piggy bank. Soon you will be looking very carefully for these tickets to see how much you can save.

  - You can reward yourself for reaching certain short savings goals. For example, if you manage to complete your tenth day without spending, you can do something fun and not too expensive for yourself or your loved ones. You can pay for a spa day for yourself and your partner, you can go out for a drink and/or lunch with a friend or you can buy something you were looking for your hobby.

  - Lower price competition. If there is an item or product that you buy consistently, the competition may be looking for the lowest price for that product in the city where you currently live. You can even compete with your partner or with a friend who buys the same until they cannot find a price lower than the last found. Then whoever found that price, wins and you can invite him to eat or whatever he wants.

- Use discount codes and coupons: However, eliminating expenses is not a matter of buying on offer, but of eliminating purchases directly. Because even if something that costs $100 gets you $70, it doesn't mean you've saved $30, it means you've spent $70. However, when you buy something, your goal should be to get the item or product you're looking for at the lowest price. Then, for items or products you buy right away, try using coupons or search for discounts. You can find coupons on various websites or constantly check magazines and newspapers so that you can find out what's on offer at various stores. Now, just use discounts and coupons for the things you really need, because it's easy to convince yourself to get that guilty taste because it's discounted now. Remember, if you feel guilty, you probably shouldn't buy it.

- Avoid shopping when you're hungry: You may have noticed that when you go home shopping, you end up buying more food than you need when you shop on an empty stomach. Most incredibly, some researchers have found that you even spend more on products that aren't necessarily food when you shop hungry. These are evolutionary reasons why one seeks to achieve more when one is hungry. So, avoid going out and buying something when you're hungry.

- Always shop with a list: Another good way to avoid impulses is to go shopping with a specific list of only what you need. The most important thing is to respect the list and not to buy things that are not included in it. The most common thing is to do this in supermarkets for home cooking, but this should also be done when you go shopping for other things. If you are going to buy clothes, write down how much and what you need. For example, 2 shirts, 2 trousers, 1 pair of shoes and a strap. So, you stay on what you're going to buy and you're going to spend less. And if you have pending purchases of products that cost a lot, try to have them written down somewhere for when an offer comes out for them.

- Unsubscribe from discount programs or offers: If you are in any of the shopping lists, coupons or offers that reach you directly to the mail, unsubscribe from those lists. While it may seem smart and a good idea to have your email list of coupons or discounts for things that interest you, the reality is that seeing offers only make you more inclined to buy something. If you really want to reduce your expenses, try to receive as few temptations as possible.

- Withdraw your credit card from accounts to buy online: If you have your credit card placed in any app or web page to make purchases, delete them from that place. Yes, it's convenient to have them there because it becomes tedious and inconvenient to have to rewrite your credit card information to buy something online. But guess what? That inconvenience is exactly the idea. If every time you want to buy something you have to put the information back in, which means taking out your wallet, looking for your card and writing the data down on the website, it makes it harder for you to buy something on impulse. Just for what you really need or want will make you take the trouble to do that. So, leave it at that. As a nuisance.

- Implement Rule 1 Inside / 1 Outside: If you already have all your fixed expenses covered, then you can apply this rule, 1 Inside / 1 Outside. What is the purpose of this rule? That every time you buy something new, boot or donate something old similar to what you're going to buy. For example, do you want a new pair of shoes? Then get rid of an old pair. And, if you don't have old shoes to throw away because they're torn or worn, then do you really need new shoes? While this won't work for everything you buy, it works for almost most daily purchases.

- Cancel unused subscriptions: You're probably spending money on things you don't need, and if you're consistently spending money on services you don't use, it's best to cancel them. Maybe it's a subscription to a magazine you really don't read much about, a subscription to the gym when you only use it for running or don't take advantage of it, a subscription to a streaming service you no longer use, etc. If you are spending on an unnecessary subscription, cancel that subscription so you can save the money you were spending on them. If you don't know which ones to cancel, make a list of all the ones you're paying for and write next to it how often you use it and ask yourself, really, which ones are worth it for the goals you've set in your life.

- Look for the total cost of any purchase: Many of the things you could buy will end up having a continuing cost or maintenance usage. For example, if you buy one of those one-cup coffeemakers, you're going to need the cups that go with it. Or a better example, if you buy a car, you will have to pay for insurance, maintenance and repairs. So, to make sure these expenses don't consume you and commit you to a lifetime of big expenses, consider how much it will cost you to maintain and operate, not just to purchase the product; especially for purchases where you use credit. For example, if you are going to pay on credit, then you must calculate how much the total of the product is going to be once you add all the interest you pay to it so that you can really consider if in the end it ends up coming out so much that it is not convenient for you and it is better to save to get it. After all, instead of paying installments, you can put the product as a short-term goal and save for it.

- Set a per-use limit: Another good way to control and reduce your expenses is to calculate a purchase with a usage limit so that you can calculate how much actual use you are giving to an item. For example, let's say your usage limit is $1. When you're looking at a product you plan to buy, think about how many times you're going to use it and divide the price by the number of uses. So, if you're thinking about buying a $500 TV that you'll use every day for the next two years, that means you'd take 730 uses out of it. You divide the price that would be $500 for $730 (remember we put a per-use limit to $1, so using it for 2 years once a day would be 730). That gives you a per-use result of $0.68 dollar cents, well below your per-use limit of $1 dollar. Then you can buy it. Just do this with the big purchases so you don't get overwhelmed. You already have several other methods for smaller purchases that don't come at such high prices.

- Plan free activities: Limiting your budget doesn't mean you have to limit your fun either. You can go to places where you know you're not going to spend much. There are free concerts in different places. You can also plan a bike ride or a walk with your partner. You can search Google for the best free activities to do in your city. If you have the beach nearby, you can walk there. Do this as an alternative to activities that make you spend a lot of money like going to the mall or a restaurant. The more you occupy your life with activities that cost nothing, the less time you'll have to spend money on things you don't need.

- Get help with your personal finances: Sometimes it's hard to be motivated to reduce your budget expenses on your own. You can make a deal with a friend or your partner so you can help each other to reduce expenses. This does not mean a punishment that your partner or friend will apply to you if you fail to spend at all. The purpose of this is to have someone to report your progress to. When you have loved ones, who care about you and encourage you, you're less likely to break your spending limits. And if you do, they should be there to understand you and help you not to do it again, just as you will help them with the same.

The One-Week Budget: Volume 2

Get One Step Closer to Financial Freedom by Creating an Easy Money Management System That Will Help You Make More Money and Keep You Debt Free

By

Income Mastery

Develop proper money management

It's important that you develop the right money management skills, with calculations and basic financial knowledge so that you can avoid falling into bankruptcy, or simply being heavily indebted even to the person who sells the newspapers on the block. You can take the following steps to develop proper money management:

- **Set priorities:** basic consumer spending is not flexible. In this case it is important to consider basic expenses such as food, health, consumption of water, electricity, gas, transportation, condominium, telephone and internet (if you work with him), minimum quality of life needs. Once this aspect has been addressed, it is essential to establish investment priorities, according to the opportunities and financial capacity in all senses, such as the availability of resources, debt option, possibilities of alliances and partnerships, capacity to pay on time, among others.

- **Don't be afraid to get into debt:** credit is a very important option for supporting people's progress, as we mentioned earlier. Be honest with the information you provide to the entity that will study your ability to pay, because this way you can establish an objective and realistic limit which you can meet your ability to pay, without affecting or drowning in rough debts that then you cannot pay. As far as possible, it uses credit only for projects that generate returns, increase capital or strengthen its productive capacity. Avoid using credit as much as possible for unnecessary consumer expenses or luxuries.

- **Distribute your money rationally:** it is important to establish the amount of your income that will be allocated to meet each of your needs and commitments and make the payment dates coincide with those of his salary to avoid arrears and interest cost overruns on arrears. Do not forget that it is always necessary to think about unforeseen events and contingencies. For contingencies, it is important to create an emergency fund to save any contingency that may arise.

- **Don't be afraid to disinvest** evaluate the opportunity to leave your investments at the right time or at the highest value. For example, if you have a property, analyze the possible development that the place may have, and do not discard its sale to use the money in another investment more profitable and equally safe. For this, you must manage a good investment plan, with a step-by-step of what to do to make it work.

- **Don't buy on impulse:** make sure that all your expenses are justified and of great importance, that is, if they are not vital, try not to make them, and save that money for more vital issues such as meals, house payments, transportation, health, etc. Any expense must have a minimum of support within the rationale of personal financial management.

- **Invest or save in education**: many studies show that the basic saving, and the most productive added value of a country, a community, a family or an individual, is education, understood as the accumulation of knowledge at the service of progress and development through productive projects. It is an added value of all communities, political trends, and much more, that help shape the way people live, always looking for the best for the person. Allocating resources to boost production capacity is fundamental in the strategy of successfully managing money at a personal or family level.

- **Do not spend more than you earn**: although this may sometimes seem a little difficult, you should be careful not to overspend your budget. Think: if you spend more money than you receive, how will you repay the debt? If you answered "borrowing", you would be borrowing a lot more, and doubling the level of difficulty getting out of debt. It is key to establish the difference between expenditure and investment: the former does not bring economic return, while the latter does, which implies that a person can increase his income by managing his money well. Only when this happens will it be possible to increase spending on other matters.

- **Economize**. The sacrifices you make today may result in benefits later.

- **Learn to distinguish between luxury and necessity.** Don't confuse needs with desires. The people who save the most, limit the purchases that are just for fun. They prefer to save with a view to achieving economic stability rather than spending on current tastes or luxuries, superficial things and luxuries.

- **Study your habits and routines.** Many people have at least one expensive habit. It can be an ordinary coffee or a cappuccino that is drunk every day, the craving for new shoes or the habit of going out to dinner. Study all your habits and routines to see what you can cut back on, so you don't spend more than you have and even have some money to save.

- **Avoid impulse purchases**. When the idea of acquiring something unforeseen comes up, give yourself a few days to think if you really need it. It's a good idea to follow the 3-day rule, which is that for all major purchases, wait three days before deciding, enough days for your enthusiasm to wane and reason to intervene, making sure that the purchase is the best option.

- **Pay with cash or debit card**. Research has shown that people are more likely to spend when they buy with a credit card, but when you want to pay with your own money, you think twice so as not to squander your monthly budget. So, if you want to control your expenses more, consider paying cash.

- **Visualize yourself reaching your goals**. If you're trying to raise a contingency fund, save money for a specific need, or even save to give yourself an unusual taste, every time you come up with the idea of making a purchase or making a decision that means spending money, think about the economic goal you've set for yourself. If the purchase in question is not going to bring you closer to your goal, ask yourself if you can do without it.

- **Enjoy the simple and free.** In life there are so many things to delight in that don't cost money. Explore and enjoy the simple, and you'll see how remarkable and enriching certain shared activities and experiences can be that are literally priceless. For example, a walk in the park, outings to the mall, family plans, among others.

- **Make a short- and medium-term personal or family budget:** this should include consumption expenses, savings portion (preferably productive), entertainment, vacations and unforeseen expenses. When it is a family budget, individual responsibilities can be assigned, according to the income of each of the members of the group, either by contributing a specific monthly amount of money or by indicating the commitment assumed by each person. For example, utilities, credit repayment, leasing, study, food, etc.

- **Save**: the money you can receive today is part of the money you'll have tomorrow. It is important to point out that there are various forms of savings, and that the most profitable is that of productive savings, that is, savings made to generate new income, in such a way that they not only conserve the value of what has been saved but also increase capital. Examples: education, housing and valuables. Don't forget that old age is an unassailable reality. Contribute to your pension. To apply for this type of savings, it is important that you have a minimum of preparation to develop it correctly.

- **Be clear about the difference between spending and investment**: spending is that activity that involves the outflow of money with no economic return. Some of the expenditures produce returns represented in happiness and quality of life, but these should only be made when general economic circumstances permit. Remember that the investment is one whose main objective is to generate a return, where you can receive a number of dividends free of expenses.

- **When it comes to investing** get the best possible advice. Although the investment is intended to generate a return, a bad decision can put you at risk and cause the opposite effect. Don't concentrate your investments on a single option, unless you're just starting the dynamic. Diversification is a way to reduce exposure to risk.

- **Do not exceed the limit of indebtedness**: unless the money you borrow is to take advantage of or undertake in a business that generates good dividends and good profitability (cost-opportunity), avoid indebtedness. Financial institutions consider that, on average, an individual or family should not be indebted to more than 30 percent of their fixed income, as this can cause an imbalance in their economy and bring problems.

Following these recommendations will help you respect and take better care of your money, as well as manage your debts correctly. A debt-free person is a happy person because he or she is not accountable to anyone, has no financial commitments to make, and mentally allows you to think of new and better financial growth strategies for yourself.

What are SMEs?

SMEs are small and medium-sized enterprises that seek their financial independence, following the examples of the large national and transnational corporations of each country. They are independent companies that seek to establish a place in the trade market, being excluded from the industrial market because they do not have large investments, which characterize the industrial market. For this reason, an SME will never be able to exceed certain annual sales or a certain number of staff.

SMEs are a great strategy to get out of debt without having to become big investors, and for that, you can follow the following tips (with reference information from the portal Buenos Negocios):

Seven keys to developing SMEs with friends

Running a small or medium business has a lot of responsibility, as much as running a mega corporation, so it is important and advisable to run a business with friends who are experts in strategic areas within the company. To develop an SME, you must:

1. **Have (and maintain) joint objectives.** There are countless reasons why someone starts a business. In addition to money and economic aspects, drivers such as personal development, growth possibilities, global problem solving, time

flexibility, fame, among others, tend to be added. If you're going to start a business with friends, it's essential to talk about each one's expectations. What are they looking for? What would be the "ideal business" model for each one? What do they want to prioritize? What do they imagine in a few years? What do they consider "success" or "failure" of the business? Once underway, doing at least an annual review of these questions will allow the team to keep aligned or adjust as necessary, without accumulating tensions that may affect the day to day.

2. **"Clear beads..."** While it may not be the main driver for some entrepreneurs, money is always a central part of any project. To preserve friendship, it is essential to be orderly and talk about economic and financial issues: what and how each will contribute to the initial investment of the business, what income they will have, who will handle the money, and so on. It is not only a matter of making informal agreements, but also of reflecting this in formal aspects, such as the composition of the society, the possession of goods and the participation in profits (and losses). If they do not have experience or specialized training, an accountant can help organize these aspects.

3. **Are we all replaceable?** One of the theoretical principles of organizations is that all people can be replaced. However, when a group of friends starts a business it is partly because they want to work with their group of membership, and this can be one of their differentiators from their competitors: teams that already know each other tend to work better and are more motivated to overcome natural obstacles in starting and growing a business.

4. **Establish a "friendship protocol".** Just as well-managed family businesses have a family protocol that establishes the rules of operation in the face of the complexity of the work and family relationship, something similar can be done between friends. We recommend that you prepare a document with some basic guidelines that can serve as a guide in difficult situations in the company (entry of partners, distribution of responsibilities, conflict resolution mechanisms, sale of the business, etc.). Talking with time and without pressure on these issues then facilitates decisions and avoids frictions that could damage the friendship.

5. **Emotions versus efficiency.** Don't let one of the characteristics influence more than the other, that is, if there are more emotions than efficiency, the business won't have the maturity to advance, and if it has more efficiency than

emotion, you won't have time to feel and know what your business needs to improve. The two dimensions must coexist in a delicate balance so that business does not stagnate, or friendship deteriorates.

6. "Mentor, coach, therapist, organizational psychologist, consultant... Searching for someone outside the business to help maintain "difficult conversations" can be a way to facilitate the relationship and decision making.

7. **Enjoy the day to day.** Find ways to take advantage of the work environment to nurture friendship and have fun: lunches, meetings, business trips, New Year's Eve parties, among others.

The idea of getting together among friends to form business strategies is that they can have fun and grow together in a joint project.

Now, we cannot forget another great strategy to apply in the development of an SME and refers to the practice of using electronic checks. The digital world is advancing, and companies are forced to apply changes and updates to their platforms and ways of working in order not to become obsolete in their different markets. Digital checks can greatly facilitate a company's banking and financial operation.

Like wire transfers, electronic checks are a great tool, because you no longer need paper money to exchange goods and do business, something that is becoming unnecessary for people.

According to the Buenos Negocios portal, the new electronic checks, or Echeqs, entered into force in Argentina in July 2019, following Central Bank regulations. These are electronic documents circulating only through digital channels and constituting payment orders from an issuer with a current account at a bank, so that a legitimate recipient or bearer can cash the amount detailed in the cheque. Although their use is not mandatory for the time being, they are expected to gradually replace the physical cheque, with the same legal backing.

Like traditional cheques, Echeqs are issued from current accounts, although they can also be deposited for collection at savings banks, and pay the tax on bank credits and debits, as recently specified by AFIP. Initially, they can only be cashed by bankers, depositing them in their accounts, although it is expected that in the future, they may also be cashed over the counter like some paper checks.

Among its advantages, it is possible to emphasize that:

- The issuance, endorsement, negotiation and general circulation operations are simplified, as all these steps are carried out through digital channels (they are broadcast and "signed" through electronic banking).

- Checks have no limits on the number of endorsements, that is, third-party checks can be used to make payments and be transferred to different recipients.

- They have a lower operating cost than traditional checks, as they reduce the need to move and verify documents.

- They are safer and more effective by reducing the likelihood of counterfeiting, adulteration or the loss or theft of checkbooks.

- Many of the reasons for rejecting checks are reduced, especially those related to formal aspects (such as erroneous account numbers, illegible information, date errors, etc.).

- As they are easier to negotiate and verify, it is simpler to use them as a form of financing, through the assignment or sale of documents.

Once this strategy is developed and understood, we embark on the 8 keys to manage payments. This management helps us to reduce many financial commitments such as payroll payment to your employees, your suppliers, and any other creditor of the company. As the company grows, the activities and amounts to be paid for operations and everything related to the maintenance of the company increase, something that can generate headaches if it is not paid on time and if a suitable financial and work model is not developed so that it works automatically. Payments are a central aspect of the operational wheel of any business and, in order to make them efficiently, it is necessary to follow some good practices:

- Consider your payments as a key aspect of your financial planning. Keep track of your commitments and operations, track and analyze data, and make informed decisions.

- Select the most efficient payment method for each case. There are many ways to make payments, each with different risks, costs and practicality: checks, deposits and bank transfers, payment services to suppliers, payment to collectors, cash. Evaluate the legal requirements and usual practices in your area and sector to decide the best form of payment in each case.

- Sets a payment schedule. Even if you handle few operations, it is easier to devote one day per week or fixed schedule to the management of payments.

- Manages one or more small boxes for minor or unforeseen expenses.

- Keep your cash flow up to date, to anticipate money needs or surpluses. Be clear about the difference between perceived and accrued criteria. In particular, schedule payment dates for issued checks to avoid the costs of rejected checks.

- Avoid the hidden costs of thinking only in the short term. It's not about plugging holes and going out to get money when you have to pay. For a comprehensive financial analysis, especially in a context of inflation, you need to consider the generation of interest on delinquencies on outstanding invoices and the cost of borrowing if you are going to use the bank overdraft to make payments.

- Think beyond money. Payments are often a key aspect of the relationship with employees, suppliers and others, and therefore their timely compliance can impact more than financially. Prioritize the payment of wages and salaries to keep your team motivated, pay your key suppliers first and be sure to consider the impact of your decisions on your future relationship.

- Internal control. Managing the money that goes out of business is a sensitive aspect; be sure to take the basic steps to avoid out-of-control and temptations. For example, it separates the tasks of preparing payments from those of moving money; it performs surprise arcades and rotates the staff who handle the money. A consultant or your accountant can help you set up safe circuits and establish control mechanisms.

It is very important to maintain control and care in all the businesses you wish to undertake or start developing. A constant monitoring of all the procedures of your company will allow you to foresee an unforeseen event and correct it in time, or simply avoid it, so that when you act on the matter, it is no longer too late. You must consider that creating your own business will not make you a millionaire quickly, unless you win the lottery, but that would not be entrepreneurship, but chance, so you must have patience to begin to see the great results of it. This is an overview of the main personal finance concepts you should consider, especially if you are an entrepreneur:

- **Your starting point conditions you.** Some come to their own business with ample personal and family funds, while others come only with their talent, enthusiasm and good ideas. In any case, it is true that there are entrepreneurs who start with nothing, and go very far, while others with huge investments like that do not find success. However, the initial finances impact not only on how much personal money you can invest in the business but also on the level of risk you can assume and the support you have in case of need or failure.

- **For entrepreneurs it is even more difficult to have an accurate diagnosis of personal finances.** With a little order, a worker in a dependency relationship can be clear about how much he generates and how much he spends, how much he contributes to his retirement and how much he is retained monthly for social work and other benefits. For an independent worker or business owner, on the other hand, accounts are not that simple. It's easy to lose control with so much going on around you: money tied up in business assets or working capital, irregular entrepreneurial income, business debts and commitments, money from partners and investors, and even large sums circulating even when the business is not profitable. It is vital to make periodic evaluations to know how much personal money you really have, and how much of that may be available in case of need. An accountant can advise you if you have any doubts.

- **Separate (and ordered) accounts reduce risks.** On the one hand, it tries to separate the accounts of the business from those of its owner, because sometimes they tend to mix in the day to day. This involves not only keeping the register independently but ensuring that the business is formally constituted as an entity separate from its owners. On the other hand, if there is more than one partner or if it is a family business, it is necessary to be ordered to reflect reality. It is common, for example, for some commercial goods to be placed in the name of family members, or for family members to use a company vehicle or spend money on behalf of the business. As long as everything flows, maybe nothing happens. But at some critical personal (e.g. divorce) or business (e.g. labor lawsuit) moment, disorder can pay dearly.

- **Align expectations and reality**. Some look for a way to earn a lot of money in their own business, others focus on creating a job that they like and that gives them freedom. Some seek to revolutionize the world, while others measure recognition only in economic results. Working as a family, having flexible hours or making your own decisions are some of the additional benefits of self-employment. Being clear about what you are looking for in entrepreneurship and what you want to receive in return, putting everything in the balance, will help you to enjoy your entrepreneurial path.

- **The extra effort of women entrepreneurs.** Women who choose to turn to their own business often face additional barriers in addition to the challenges typical of any entrepreneur. Access to financial education and personal money management are some of the most recent challenges on the road to gender equity.

- **Everyone who undertakes it hopes that it will go well,** however, is not the reality for many, so not only must be mentally prepared to overcome the failure, but also must organize the accounts to be able to move forward in case of need. The general recommendation, for entrepreneurs and non-entrepreneurs, is to maintain a readily available reserve fund, with money to survive at least six months without income. It will allow you to reorganize and try again or get a job in the meantime.

- **Managing growing wealth is also a challenge**. An additional tip if you have the luck and ability to be among those who through your own business come to wealth, is to learn to manage your wealth and manage it so that you can maximize the growth of your business and your personal development.

A good strategy to guarantee your financial future with your ventures is to follow all the strategies mentioned above. But if your business operates a point of sale to accept debit and credit cards, it's critical to know what chargebacks are, why they can be generated, and how to claim to recover the money from that sale when possible.

A chargeback is a debit that the administrator or financial entity of the credit card makes to the merchant on a transaction that had already been paid and arises from a claim of the issuing bank or the cardholder in question.

The characteristics of a chargeback are as follows:

- **Countercharges for lack of knowledge of purchase:** it happens when the client says he did not make that purchase, it can happen because he does not recognize the operation in the summary of the bank. There are measures that trade can take to avoid chargebacks for this reason.

- **Rejections: the** operation was not accepted by the card, for some error the purchase was not processed. To retrieve these coupons, the only option is to contact the customer. This is why it is essential to have your data.

- **Return: a** customer made a purchase; the card was paid for and then the customer requested the return. In these cases, the card makes a chargeback for return.

- **Chargeback for duplicate sales:** if for some reason the card receives the same coupon twice, it generates a chargeback for one of them. If both have been processed from the POS terminal and both are signed by the customer, the card holder must pay them and both charges are made.

- **Promotional chargeback:** when a bank arranges a promotion with the trade and pays the full sale, it makes a promotional chargeback to discount what they had agreed to. These chargebacks are not claimable.

But this should not worry you, because here we will recommend three strategies to avoid chargebacks:

1. **Always ask for the document next to the card and check the data.** The main tool available to the trade to claim a chargeback is the signed coupon. That's why you should always ask for the document next to the card and check the data, that the photo matches the person who is making the purchase and that the signature of the card and the coupon are not very different. In the latter case, it is preferable to cancel the coupon and reprint it for the customer to sign again. You can also help avoid chargebacks by having the merchant record the customer's document and phone number, rather than asking the customer to write it down. This way the trade is sure to understand the letter and not lose the data.

2. **Trying to make the company name and fantasy name similar.** One of the most common reasons for refusals is the difficulty in associating the fantasy name of the trade with the business name that appears on credit card statements. Whenever possible, the name next to which the customer is going to observe the amount of the purchase in the summary, should be equally or easily related to that of the trade.

3. **Products in good condition and friendly customer service.** The third key has to do with people's experience in commerce. Customer service is extremely important in many respects, even to avoid chargebacks. Also, the quality of the products and the state in which they are stored. The control of stock (quantity of goods) helps to optimize these resources and that customers leave the premises satisfied. When this does not happen, they may be unaware of purchases as a form of protest and, if they do not have the documentation mentioned above, they lose time and money.

What to do and how to react to a chargeback?

As recommended by the Buenos Negocios agency, specialized in business finance, from the day the commerce receives the liquidation, it has a period of time to make any type of claim that depends on each credit card.

After that time, the settlement is considered consensual and any right to challenge is lost and there will no longer be any way to recover the money debited from the sale that suffered the chargeback. It is fundamental that the commerce controls the sales with cards to find out in time of the chargebacks of your business and to be able to make the claims every time that corresponds, this is the most advisable thing to carry out the claim, which varies according to each card. Step one is to locate the coupon signed by the customer and scan it.

Already developed all the strategies to undertake in an SME, it is also important to plan well in advance your retirement or retirement, because obviously you do not want to work or be at the forefront of your business for life, although perhaps at this time say yes, when the time comes you might regret that thinking.

Therefore, some actions you can take right now to start planning that big step, even if you prefer not to think about leaving your venture, are:

- **Register and pay contributions with your future in mind.** You can't just count on an official retirement to fund retirement years. Although the payment of self-employed workers, and the payment of monotax to a lesser extent, imply contributions that count for calculating future retirements in the state system, generally these are amounts of retirements that are going to be significantly lower than the usual income of an entrepreneur, and that of their peers in a relationship of dependency. In many cases, moreover, entrepreneurs work in the informal sector without making such contributions, and therefore have difficulty accessing the system. Find out your situation with an accountant: years of contributions, retirement you could access, registration options to improve your future income, and so on.

- **Separate personal and business money.** A common mistake of many entrepreneurs is to mix individual or family goods and money with those belonging to the commercial activity. Put all the accounts in order, this represents a great step to understand with how much accounts for retirement, or to know the value of the business in case of sale or transfer.

- **Estimate retirement needs and financial possibilities.** How much money will you need per month when you are no longer working?

What would you like to do in retirement years? What part can come from retirement and what part from savings or liquidation of assets? Think that to your normal expenses and projected activities you will probably have to add medical and care expenses, as well as expenses that today you can have covered from the business. If projected accounts don't close, be sure to start saving to make the future you envision a reality.

- **Put together a business retirement plan**. It's not just about doing the math; it's also important to establish the steps you're going to take to leave the business: what role do you want, and can you keep? When would you like to leave the activity? What happens if you get sick and are forced to leave the business unexpectedly?

- **Plan the succession, transfer or sale of the business**. Some entrepreneurs choose to always be close to their business and keep working, while others prefer to put an end to and enjoy retirement free of work-related occupations. In both cases it is necessary to prepare it is not easy to organize the succession of the family business, the transfer to a third party or the sale of a business or goodwill.

If you have a successful financial history and believe it's time for your business to jump-start and grow, it's time to know how much money you could earn through credit that helps you maximize your wealth. Credit, if well used, can be a growth engine for small and medium-sized enterprises. These are not only loans, but there are various forms of financing offered by financial system institutions, such as corporate cards and account overdrafts.

If you want to apply for a loan, you must take into account a number of factors, because, on the one hand, those who lend the money evaluate some formal aspects, for example, how your company is legally constituted, who are its partners and what is the history of the company. On the other hand, aspects related to the development of the business are considered, such as, for example, how you are going to apply the money ordered and how your projections improve due to the use of credit.

You should consider the following scenarios, based on the requirements usually requested by local banks, to understand how much credit and what type of credit you can access, depending on the stage of business your company is in:

1. **Start-up companies.** There are some lines of credit to promote the formation of new companies, although it is not easy to obtain formal loans for businesses that do not show a certain trajectory. Check if your project meets the necessary requirements to qualify for these incentives.

2. **Companies that are not formally incorporated**. Lack of formality or independent registration are often barriers to obtaining business financing. You can get money in the form of personal loans, which are usually more expensive than those oriented toward formally incorporated businesses.

3. **Individuals with commercial activity.** Some professionals, traders and service providers of a certain size may have a significant turnover, even if they operate under a registration as natural persons. This usually entitles them to special lines of credit, which may include credit cards, overdrafts and loans that may be backed by pledges or require certain guarantees.

4. **Formally constituted companies, with basic file.** If your company is a SA (corporation) or SRL (limited liability company) only with minimal documentation and meeting certain background requirements, it is possible to receive basic financing in the form of overdraft agreements, purchase of corporate checks and credit cards. For this purpose, the presentation of the copy of the last balance sheet, the social contract or statute, the powers granted by the company, the acts of appointment of authorities, among other requirements that will depend on the financial entity where you will apply for credit. As for the background, the credit history

is evaluated, in particular, that there are no delinquent debts in other banks, or have pension debt, or tax executions in force, among other aspects.

5. **Formally incorporated companies, with complete documents.** If you can add more balances (two previous years minimum), to the information and background of the previous point evolution of sales, projections of the business with and without financing, and other documents that show a solid case, you will have access to a better rating that allows you to receive more money. To the instruments mentioned in the previous point, fully rated companies may have access to financial loans, in some cases for specific purposes, such as equipment.

If you already have a business, it's important to control card sales, even if it's a complex task. Some of the reasons that can make this activity difficult are the following:

- It is important to log in every day to download the settlement and review chargebacks.

- Liquidations are often not friendly or easy to understand.

- To make use of the data you need to manually pass it to Excel.

For this reason, experts indicate that lack of control over card payments is very common. Many card merchants do not have visibility into their cash flow, which is one of the main indicators of the merchant's financial condition. This affects trade because it prevents it from planning. It is essential to have projected revenues and expenditures on hand to make better decisions and to know the real possibilities of meeting payment commitments or to know how an investment will impact cash flow projection.

You can lose a lot of money for these situations:

- **Rejections and chargebacks that are not claimed on time**: chargebacks are debits that administrators make on operations that have already been paid. In some cases, they can be claimed, but if the trade doesn't know it and doesn't do it in time it loses that money.

- **Delays in accreditation:** due to lack of control, merchants may not perceive a delay in the deposits they must receive for their credit and debit card sales. Any error in this process is difficult to see without the right tools.

- **Loss of money due to unclear cash flow**: many businesses advance payments because they are uncertain about the amounts that will be credited to their accounts or about the deadlines.

This generates financial costs that can be avoided.

- **Non-Recoverable Withholding**: A percentage of the cost of card sales is tax and withholding. If this amount is accounted for correctly, it can be recovered, and the tax credit maximized. Lack of clarity causes businesses to lose sight of it, not process it correctly, and then it becomes a cost they could avoid.

For this reason, experts suggest using a tool to automate this complex process of card sales control, and thus have accurate information taken from the card administrators and ordered to have a clear picture of the money that will come from sales each day, without the need to re-check coupons by hand.

Common mistakes made during the use of money

Many people make countless mistakes when it comes to using money, which means that at the end of the month they are very short of it, however, if you take into account and become aware of these errors, you can control and use your money in a more effective way.

A study conducted by the Intersectoral Commission for Economic and Financial Education in Colombia found that these are the most common mistakes people make when handling their money:

- 94% of respondents reported that they planned their budget, but only 23% knew exactly when they had spent the previous week.

- 88% of adults expressed concern about having to face higher expenses in the future (e.g. retirement).

- Only 41% have plans to pay for their old-age expenses, and only 1 in 5 could afford the significant unforeseen expenses.

- Those consulted have high scores in the knowledge of simple economic and financial concepts, but a smaller proportion have correct answers in the estimation of the simple or compound interest rate, or on the knowledge of bank deposit insurance, which are concepts that eventually allow better financial decisions to be made.

- People have a high orientation to the present, for example, they say "I'd rather spend money than save for the future", a popular phrase among savers.

- In terms of expenditure control and savings, approximately 60% of all adults carry a budget, control their expenditure and save on a daily basis, although most do so outside the financial system.

Once some of the main mistakes made by people have been detected, you can follow a series of recommendations to improve your financial status. Among the recommendations are:

- **Make a budget**: you should have a clear relationship of how much money goes into your pocket and how much you are spending. If you manage household accounts, you should be very responsible for the money you put in and what you're getting into. There can be no waste, and for that, it is useful to classify it in items such as education, housing, entertainment and transportation, among others.

- **Learn to say 'NO'**: many times, an occasional outing, a birthday, a social celebration represents a monetary quota that was not counted in the monthly, weekly or daily budget. Then the best thing is to say, "for next time" or "this time I can't".

- **Get out of debt:** when there is no income and bills are overdue, the solution to illiquidity is to borrow from someone. If you are forced into debt, remember to have additional income to pay your obligations. That way you'll save money and disgust.

- **Invest:** Once you've accumulated some money from your savings, it's time to put them to work.

- **Plan**: In most cases, we can identify income and expenses that are approaching, either short-term, such as job bonuses or Christmas gifts, or long-term, such as retirement. Establish a financial plan for these events, don't leave it to chance or to last minute.

- **Paying on time:** being 'good pay' is your best letter of introduction in the financial system, do not leave the payment of your public or private bills for the last day, as this habit makes you more likely to go into default or fall behind with your obligations.

- **Protect:** no one has the future bought, look for mechanisms that help minimize the economic impacts of fortuitous situations such as earthquakes, traffic accidents or disease.

- **Acquire financial education**: empower yourself with your relationship to the financial system and understand how it can support you in achieving your goals.

Your way of thinking must change to avoid the financial hemorrhages in your life, because with these recommendations you can stop and avoid many economic problems with families, providers, and more. If you are still not convinced of these techniques, we recommend 5 simple steps to get out of debt:

1. **Mentality.** That thought that makes you feel an emotion that leads you to act in a certain way and get a result. Simply decide to buy your freedom by getting out of debt and act accordingly.

2. **Keeps a Record of Expenses.** In order to get rid of your loans and credit cards, you may need to improve and control your personal finances. You have to know how much you make and what you spend it on. If you have to save to use that money (or part of it) to get out of debt, you will have to know exactly on which items you spend the money. Write down your expenses and once a month analyze where your money has

gone, this will allow you to make concrete and accurate decisions about which expenses you are going to reduce or do without to reach your goal of ending your debts.

3. **He scores and orders**. Write down all your debts, and not just your bank debts, for example, if a relative of yours ever lent you money, if you owe any term of a purchase of greater amount, write them on a sheet and put it somewhere visible, this will allow you to be focused on your goal. If you add a photograph of something you want to do (a trip, for example) once you get out of debt, your motivation will be strengthened.

4. **Act**. It orders the debts of the previous item by time from lowest to highest. The ones you have the least time left to finish will be the first you must attack. Allocate the monthly savings you make after detecting money leaks in step 2 with your spending control and dedicate that amount to paying off the debt that appears first on your list in advance. When you're done with it, use the monthly savings plus the installment of the finished debt and go for debt number 2 on your list. Cancel debt number 2 on your list early with that money.

5. **Accelerates the process with extra income**. If it is a common and current income of those who exchange your time for money (on behalf of

others or as self-employed) does not work, because you would fall into the paradox of being even more slave, the ideal is that you implement a passive income, the one you want.

Boost your debt-free living strategy

You can live with the philosophy of living debt free. It is preferable that you live inhibiting yourself of luxuries, but calm and without debts, than spending more and suffering at the end of the month looking for the money to pay off your debts. To live debt free, you must follow these simple steps:

1. **Understand what kind of loans you have.** There are many ways to understand what a problem is, however, the first step in solving this will always be to define it. When we think about how to get out of debt, we usually do so out of the urgency of the day-to-day, the dissatisfaction with the feeling that you're only working to cover loan payments, or the anguish of living up to the thought of what juggling we'll do to make credit card payments this month, as we discussed earlier. If you really want to live without loans, the first thing you should do is have the broadest and clearest possible view of your financial situation to give it the urgency and importance it really requires. Doing so can be uncomfortable and generate fear and anxiety because it involves facing the result of many decisions you have made in the past consciously or unconsciously, but it will be a necessary encounter to have if your deepest longing is to generate real change in the way we are managing our money and fulfilling our deepest objectives. Thus, the first

step is to make a list as detailed as possible with the following information:

- **Who do I owe?** We are referring to the name of the person or to the name of the financial entity.

- **How much do I owe you?** In other words, the total value of the debt as of today. In other words, what you should pay him today if he wanted to wake you up tomorrow without that loan.

- **How much do I pay you each month?** In other words, the value of the share of the credit. If the fee is daily, weekly, or biweekly, just multiply it by the number of days, weeks, or fortnights in the month to find the total monthly payments you must make on that debt.

- **How long will it take for you to pay?** That is, the number of months remaining to leave that credit if you continued to pay your normal dues.

- **What effective annual interest rate do you charge me?** I mean, the percentage I have to pay every year to get that loan.

- **What would be a brief history of that debt?** What was the situation that encouraged or forced you to acquire that credit, and the decision process you followed to choose that loan?

2. Measure the impact these loans have on your personal finances

Not all loans have the same impact on your personal finances, in principle, because a consumer credit (credit card, free investment, etc.) is not comparable to a credit that was used for the purchase of long-term assets (mortgage or vehicle, for example), or against an informal credit (drop by drop, daily pay). Secondly, because there are credits with much higher quotas than others. Third, because they have different interest rates and annual costs, among others. Finally, because the habits that each of us has towards a debt end up conditioning their impact on our economy.

- **Assess your level of solvency:** When we talk about solvency, we mean the ability we have to meet our obligations based on the things we have, that is, what we want to know is whether the total value of our assets would be sufficient to cover our debts. As long as your total assets are higher than your total debts, you can say that you are financially solvent. However, when the value of your assets is less than the total of your debts, it can be said that you are not financially solvent.

- **Assess your level of liquidity**: In finance, when we talk about liquidity, we mean having enough cash to be able to meet the payments and obligations that we have to make on a day-to-day basis. Evaluating our liquidity level is very simple, for this, it is enough to compare the total value that we pay monthly in credit fees against our net income and our expenses. If you're too moderate or savvy when it comes to spending, it's possible that dividing your total installment payments by your total net income will result in a number greater than 0.3 (or 30%) indicating that you're facing liquidity problems.

Last but not least, Harvard University developed a fairly effective method of getting out of debt.

This method consists of prioritizing all debts with smaller balances, rather than focusing on obligations with higher interest rates. It seems a setback, because how is it better to pay the smallest balance and neglect those with the highest balance and higher interest rates?

According to the portal expansión.com, this is a system focused on reducing debt, both for individuals, natural person, as well as companies and businesses. The 'snowball method' was born from the research of several members of the Harvard Business Review.

For the methodology, an experiment was carried out in which several participants had to simulate the virtual payment of their debts. After obtaining the results, the authors of the study concluded that the factor that had the greatest impact was not the amount remaining to be paid, that is to say, the remaining debt, but the amount that they had managed to get rid of once paid.

If you analyze this conclusion, you probably infer that it makes more sense to pay bills with higher interest rates first, but you should think beyond that. People tend to be more confident and hopeful when they realize that part of their obligations are being eliminated no matter how small. In other words, focusing on paying off debts with lower interest rates tends to have a much more effective effect on the progress of total debt reduction.

How is the 'snowball method' used?

By decomposing Sall's spreadsheet, it is possible to use the method. It basically consists of:

- **Calculate economic capacity**: Help organize yourself with different Excel apps and templates to keep track of your income, expenses and debts. The greater the economic effort you make now to get rid of the debt, the less you will have to pay later, and therefore the sooner you will reach stability.

- **Plan:** Once you've done that, you have to figure out how much you can afford to spend on the higher debts. The idea is to see if you have the capacity to spend a greater amount each month to pay for them.

- **Pay:** You should write down and create a spreadsheet which includes all the debts you have, those that are smaller at the beginning and finally, the largest. It must include the interest rate for each of them and the minimum monthly payment for them. With this calculation you will see how many months you will have to dedicate to the payment of the debts until you manage to eliminate them completely.

Now, there are ten things you must do to get out of your debts, which are:

3. **Accept your debt**: Like any addiction, the first step to ending your addictions is to accept it. Therefore, you should begin by knowing the total amount of your debt and be determined to end it. To achieve this, you can do the following: write down and remember '**I'm going to get out of debt**', make a chart that allows you to see how much you are missing, share your situation with someone else, and don't try to hide it.

4. **Always negotiate your debt**: If you start negotiating in everything you do; it will be easier to save a good amount of money. In the case of debts, you can access entities that offer a portfolio purchase, this will help you lower interest, time payments and be more committed to the goal to achieve.

5. **Spend all your money to pay debts:** During a good time, you will have to make great sacrifices to be able to spend a larger amount for the payment of debts. Start by lowering the amount of luxury and unnecessary things you frequent in your life. You should also look for new income, with the goal of increasing your money and paying off the debt faster.

6. **Change your hobbies:** Try to leave the dependence on paid services like television, cell phone plans and restaurants, and learn to appreciate what you have and what you really

need. Do a study of what you really need and stay only with the basics, because saving a little money here can make a difference.

7. **Learn about money**: Spend time learning how to better manage your money. Today, there are a host of tools that will help you improve your financial health, including courses, conferences, expert assistance, counseling, and much more.

8. **Keep in mind the power of 'No'**: Remember you can always say no. Don't get involved in projects where you won't win something. Always make decisions that fit your plans and discard anything that won't do you any good. As well as saving on unnecessary expenses such as pay TV services, phone rents, and more, the money saved here will also be very helpful to you.

9. **Live with less**: Be more aware of what you really need to live and remember 'less is more'. Consumerism can be the best friend of financial institutions and the worst enemy of debtors, as they are increasingly indebted to financial institutions to pay those luxuries.

10. **Sell what's left over:** If you have items that you don't use and they're in good condition, sell them. This will help you earn extra income and meet the above goal.

11. **Use the cash to pay** If you are one of those who used the credit and you are in debt for it, better use the cash. This will help you put a realistic budget in place and limit yourself if you feel the need to overspend.

12. **Cook**: Eating out is really expensive. Therefore, try to prepare your food, you will see that your pocket and health will improve.

Conclusion

There are many factors that can positively and negatively influence your credit history, which can be fatal if you don't know how to use it to your advantage and can be very beneficial to you if you study every move well. As we say throughout this book, the main key is to avoid assuming debts that exceed the amount of your income, because logically you will not have how to pay off those debts in the future, and even worse, it will be very difficult to assume the costs of interest generated by the time the payment is late. If you are a person with financial intelligence, you will see that you can use this option in your favor, because you can apply for credits to create your own business or entrepreneurship that generates enough dividends to pay off your debts, and also generate that this money and business work for you, thus leaving the so difficult world of debts.

Correct all financial mistakes and bad vices that are part of your life by following the tips explained above. Avoid financial hemorrhaging, phantom expenses, such as continuing to pay for Gym membership, even if you don't go for lack of time, or you only go 2 days out of the 5 days you pay. You can lead a debt-free life with simple tips and strategies, plus measure the impact the loans you apply for make on your personal finances.

Now, if you are a person with a successful credit history, the bank will be the first one interested in increasing your credit limits so that you apply for them for use, but beware, because, although it may be beneficial for one party, it is a double-edged sword for the other. It is beneficial for the bank to increase your credit limits and for you to use them, because that generates more interest in favor of the financial entity, money that enters the bank for its maintenance, and that to tell the truth, that is the real business of the banks, but it can be dangerous for the applicant who is sometimes able to pay off, but may have other times where it is more complicated to do so, but if he uses it in a more intelligent way, as applying for loans to invest in his own business, or acquisitions that generate dividends, it can be very attractive and beneficial to him.

In summary, credits are a great strategy and financial tool used for the neediest, but also, for the entrepreneur who decides to devote himself to this business, the important thing is to participate in this in an intelligent way, with sufficient training and being advised by experts in the matter.

The One-Week Budget: Volume 3

Get One Step Closer to Financial Freedom by Creating an Easy Money Management System That Will Help You Make More Money and Keep You Debt Free

By

Income Mastery

Types of Budgets

There are different types of budgets, so you can select one according to your lifestyle or need, among them we can find the following:

Traditional Budgeting

This was the first technique to be used; it emerged in the public sector to guarantee citizens an honest administration of public resources. This budget is based primarily on a control criterion, which seeks to prevent those who manipulate funds from using them for purposes other than those approved or traced. For this reason, it is a budget made with the traditional approach that only allows and approves getting information about the things that the organization or institution will buy, in addition to the administrative units authorized to do so.

This technique is also called "incremental", since the budget calculation is based on what was appropriated in the previous period adjusted for current inflation, analyzing only new projects that are annexed, but periodic activities are not reviewed. This is a spending control tool, which seeks to measure the accounting management of money and control the integrity of spending. It is not considered a planning tool as it allocates funds to administrative units, not to fixed objectives.

Positive aspects:

1. Its classification by object of expenditure allows a broad breakdown, and therefore greater control.

2. The accounting evaluation of the management is assured.

3. It allows the verification of the administrative responsibility of the managers in charge of the management of the funds.

4. It's inexpensive, fast and simple.

Negative aspects:

Each area of work has different goals or objectives, but the amounts are not assigned to those activities directly, but to the unit or department in charge of executing the budget, so that in the end nobody knows to which goals or objectives the funds will be assigned, and it will be at the discretion of those in charge of managing the resources, even though some goals will be more important than others and some will have more prestige than others, which can be dangerous for the achievement of objectives.

As it is not a planning tool, it is not attached to the organization's plans, it moves in a budgetary inertia that increases over time, without this increase being related to the activities carried out.

It is limited to include inflation for costs and expenses corresponding to activities carried out in the previous period, annexing those that begin in the present period. It does not question the relevance of previous allocations.

1. Its purpose is not only to pursue objectives or goals, but also to avoid wastage, that is, to measure management and its probity in accounting terms.

2. It is designed to facilitate administration, accounting and auditing of accounts, follows a criterion of control of expenditure.

3. By focusing on what (what is acquired) and not on what for (what is acquired), it can result in expenditures being legally executed, but goals not being met.

4. The actions of each administrative unit are detached from an integral process of the organization.

Budget by Program (PPP)

For the United Nations, in 1966, it is a system in which particular attention is paid to the things that a government does or acquires. This budget presents the purposes and objectives for which the funds are required, the costs of the proposed programmed to achieve those objectives and the quantitative data that measure the performance or productivity achieved in each of the programmed.

In short, the Programmed Budget is a means of measuring the achievements of each programmed or objective, with management being measured as a whole. The elaboration of a PPP implies that from the general plan of the organization the specific objectives for the year in question are extracted, quantified through goals, discriminated in specific tasks and activities. When determining a task to be executed, it is possible to calculate the costs or inputs required to carry out the development of the task. Once this process has been completed, there is an annual operational plan that each administrative unit has as its mission to carry out in order to contribute to the achievement of the general objectives. With this system one never loses sight of the objective of the organization. Like many techniques that begin in the public sphere and then become generalized, PPP is a budgetary technique for any organization.

Positive aspects:

1. Enables the evaluation of the efficiency of each entity.

2. It systematically accumulates valuable information.

3. Select the best alternatives based on cost-benefit.

4. More realistic estimates, more sincerity in the figures.

5. The initiation of new programs, modification or deletion of others, is justified and not arbitrary.

6. Specific responsibilities are established for the personnel, for the execution of each program. Deviations are detected.

7. There is a better understanding of how an institution operates.

8. An orderly and systematic way of considering administrative management is established.

9. An analytical habit is created in the staff. (cost-benefit analysis and evaluation).

10. It requires a constant evaluation of the overall performance of the entire organization.

11. It really introduces the concept of planning in short-sighted countries geared towards effectiveness.

12. It introduces rationality into financial decisions.

Negative aspects:

1. It has to be in constant evaluation to adapt to the environment.

2. Many management activities are not justifiable as a measure of results.

3. The PPP measurement does not indicate quality, only quantity.

4. It doesn't guarantee better management programs on its own.

5. It is a long-term product, as a result of a change in customs and organization.

6. It does not measure complex activities. (sovereignty, stability, long-term permanence, etc.).

Zero Base Budget (ZBP).

It is a system in which budget requests start from scratch, regardless of previous assignments. Evaluates all of the organization's activities to see which should be eliminated, placed on a lower level, or increased. It seeks to counteract the effect of traditional budgets by eliminating habit allocations. It is the manager's responsibility to justify why he or she should receive a given budget. It is very expensive as it requires time for preparation and increases office work. Since time is a relevant variable in the preparation of the budget, the cost-benefit ratio may not justify its use.

It was originally developed at Texas Instruments in 1970 by Peter Phyrr, primarily for management operations. It could be said that it is a budget reengineering technique and its use can reduce up to 70% of the costs of the organization, but as any reengineering can be a traumatic process for staff, because they could present resistance to change.

Cost per activity

Its main application is basically in indirect manufacturing costs. Currently, indirect manufacturing costs have increased their influence on the total cost of the product, while direct labor has decreased, forcing the search for new distribution bases in order to improve their allocation.

The first thing to do when executing this technique is to identify the activities, then identify their costs, determine the bases of the activity for those costs, assign the costs for the activities and assign them to the products. Its implementation is a little complex, requires time, effort and money to classify operations into activities, also causes changes in the way of working and this causes rejection by workers. Additionally, it requires a permanent audit in order to verify that the activities are within the budgeted costs.

This is a cost method in which products are classified by activity and according to the type of activity in which they are included, the cost is assigned to each of them. Greater utility has been observed in companies with a diversity of processes and products, as it defines costs more precisely and can discover those that are being sold at a loss.

How can budgets be classified?

There are several criteria and points of view that allow us to classify the budget, among which we find:

According to flexibility:

- **Rigid, static, fixed or assigned**: also known as **static budget**, it is a single plan and does not make reservations for changes that may occur during the period for which it was created. It is fundamentally based on the fact that the estimates in the forecasts are correct. For example:

"The budget presented corresponds to a fixed budget, and in it an estimate is made of the quarterly and annual production of the factory of some product and, also, of sales for those periods, but no provision is made to consider possible changes in production figures or in sales estimates as a result of changes in the economic situation of the country, of increase in the prices of raw materials, etc. i.e. it considers that there will be no change.

Now, in the case of a country whose economy is not stable, fixed budgets are not the most advisable, unless they cover a relatively short period of time that allows the price not to fluctuate.

- **Flexible or variable**: they are those that are elaborated for different levels of activity and can be adapted to the different circumstances of the environment. These budgets are generally well accepted in the modern budget area. They are dynamic and adaptive, but complicated and expensive. These budgets show revenues, costs, and expenses adjusted for the size of manufacturing or commercial operations. It stands out in the budgetary field of costs, manufacturing overheads, administrative and sales. It is prepared for different types of operations or uses, providing projected information for different volumes of critical variables, especially those that represent a restriction or conditioning or risk factor. Its main characteristic is to avoid the rigidity of the master or static budget that projects a fixed or static level of work, transforming it into a dynamic tool with several levels of operation to know the impact on the expected results of each range of activity, as a consequence of the different reactions of the costs against those. This means that it is created for a certain volume between a minimum and a higher one, given by the maximum level of activity of the company.

But there are also those that are according to the period they cover:

- **Short-term**: are performed to cover the planning of the organization in the cycle of operations of one year. This system can be adapted to countries with inflationary economies.

- **Long-term: as far as possible**. correspond to the development plans generally adopted by states and large companies.

There are those that are according to the field of applicability in the company.

- **Master budget:** is the main and one of the most important budgets of a company, i.e., the end of a whole process of planning and planning, and includes all areas of business such as sales, production, purchasing, etc., and that is why it is called master. This budget, which includes all expenses, is made up of two smaller budgets: the operating budget and the financial budget.

The operating budget also consists of smaller budgets.

- **The sales budget**: it is where you foresee how much you expect to sell on that, you will know how much you should produce and how much it will cost to do so. It is important to check what raw material is needed, how much labor will be used, what the indirect costs of production will be and how much it will all cost. By knowing how much raw material is needed, you can plan and budget for purchases.

- **Operating budgets**: consist of all revenues and expenses that a company, government or organization uses to plan and coordinate its operations over a period of time, usually a quarter or a year. It is prepared before beginning an accounting period, as a goal to be achieved. Shows the company's projected revenue and associated expenses for the next period, usually next year. Generally, company management goes through the process of collecting budget data before the start of the year and then performs continuous updates each month. It may consist of a high-level summary plan, backed up by details that support each budget line.

- **Investment budgets**: represent everything in which the company or person must "Invest" for a purpose that goes beyond the fiscal year of one year. If the company is looking to grow with new products, it may need to invest in new or better machinery, if it wants to expand its ability to distribute its products, it may need new trucks or open new warehouses in other cities, or acquire, or remodel new offices, i.e., an investment is everything that normally accompanies a growth or improvement of the company. It is important to note that this budget must be accompanied by an analysis of the return that these investments will bring to the company via additional cash flow or additional profit, if it is an investment to expand operations. If it is an investment for technological improvement, perhaps the return does not come from the generation of new cash flow, but from cost savings or operating expenses that this.

Functions to be fulfilled in a budget

The budget has many functions to fulfill, but here are the most important in general terms:

- Gives complete financial control of the organization.

- Budgetary control is the process of discovering what is being done, comparing and evaluating the results with your previously budgeted data, in order to verify achievements or remedy differences.

- A budget can play both preventive and corrective roles within the organization or company.

- The budget is also useful in most organizations. Companies such as: utilitarian (business companies), non-utilitarian (government agencies), large (multinationals, conglomerates) and small businesses.

- Budgets are important because they help minimize risk in company operations.

- Through budgets, it is possible to keep the company's operational plan within reasonable limits.

- They serve as a mechanism for the revision of company policies and strategies, in order to direct them towards strategic objectives.

It should be noted that the budget is a plan of action aimed at meeting a planned or set goal, expressed in financial terms and values that must be met at a certain time and under certain conditions. This concept is applied in each center of responsibility of the organization. This is known as a document containing a generally annual forecast of income and expenditure relating to a given economic activity. A budget can usually be an annual financial plan.

- In financial terms, it quantifies the various components of its total action plan.

- Budget lines serve as guides during the implementation of staff programmed at a given time and serve as a standard of comparison once plans and programmes have been completed.

- Budgets serve as means of communication between units at a certain level and vertically between executives from one level to another. A network of budget estimates is filtered upwards through successive levels for further analysis.

The budget functions as a tool for the planning of activities, or of an action or set of actions, reflected in monetary amounts which determine in advance the lines of action to be followed in the course of a given period.

Existing Elements in a Budget

A budget is a plan that must take care of even the smallest details, because as it is the mathematics, it must be a very exact calculation of everything that must be contemplated, and for that you must take into account the following elements for the creation of a budget:

- The budget expresses what the administration will try to do, in such a way that the company achieves an upward change in a certain period.

- **Integrator:** indicates that it takes into account all areas and activities of the company. It is a plan but it is also aimed at each of the areas, in such a way that it contributes to the achievement of the overall objective. This process is known as master budget, formed by the different areas that make it up.

- **Coordinator:** means that the plans for several of the company's departments must be prepared jointly and in harmony. If these plans are not coordinated, the master budget will not equal the sum of the parts and will create confusion and error.

- In financial terms, it highlights the importance that the budget must be represented in the monetary unit to serve as a means of communication, otherwise problems would arise at the time of analyzing the master plan.

- **Operations:** One of the fundamental objectives of a budget is to determine the income to be obtained, as well as the expenses to be produced. This information should be as detailed as possible.

- **Resources:** it is not enough to determine future expenses and revenues; the company must also plan the resources necessary to carry out its operating plans, which is basically achieved with financial planning, which includes the cash budget and the budget for asset additions (inventories, accounts receivable, fixed assets).

- Within a certain future period, a budget always has to be in function of a certain period.

According to some studies, companies that use budgets carry out four aspects:

1. They commit themselves to the budget.

2. They connect short term planning with medium- and long-term planning.

3. They adopt detailed and understandable procedures for making budgets.

4. They analyze budget variations and take corrective action.

A Company's Revenue Budget Process

This activity quantitatively reflects the objectives set by the company in the short term, through the timely establishment of programs, without losing the perspective of the long term, as this will condition the plans that the company or organization has with a specific purpose. The process consists of the following steps:

1. Definition and transmission of the general guidelines to those responsible for preparing the budgets.

2. Elaboration of plans, programs and budgets.

3. Negotiation of budgets.

4. Coordination of budgets.

5. Approval of budgets.

6. Monitoring and updating of budgets.

Most Outstanding Budgets

For its recurrent use in a company, venture, or organization, outstanding budgets are as follows:

- **Production Budget**

These are estimates that are closely related to the sales budget and desired inventory levels. The production budget is actually the sales budget projected and adjusted by the change in inventory, first we must determine whether the company can produce the amounts projected by the sales budget, in order to avoid an exaggerated cost in the labor occupied. For this, it is important to highlight the following components: Miscellaneous personnel, Number of hours required, Value per unit hour.

- **Manufacturing Expense Budget**

They are estimated budgets of direct or indirect form that intervene in all the stages of the production process, they are expenses that must be charged to the cost of the product. It is important to consider a Maintenance Expense budget, which also impacts manufacturing expenses. This includes man-hours required, operation of machines and equipment, stock of accessories and lubricants.

- - **Production Cost Budget**

They are estimated budgets that specifically intervene in the whole process of unitary manufacture of a product, it means that of the total of the budget of the requirement of materials the required quantity must be calculated by type of line produced the same one that must agree with the budget of production.

Characteristics:

- Only the materials required for each line or mold should be considered.

- The cost must be estimated.

- Not all require the same materials.

- The value must match the unit cost established in the production cost.

- **Quotation for material requirements**

This allows the quantity to be established on a basic established for each type of product, as well as the amount of capital budgeted for each area, must respond to production requirements, the procurement department must establish the program to be coupled with the production budget, if there is a need for a greater requirement, will take the flexibility of the first budget for a timely expansion and thus meet production requirements. It is important to verify the variations of the international markets, to find the best point of purchase.

- **Administrative Expenditure Budget**

It is considered the core and most important part of any budget, as most of it is earmarked. They are estimates that cover the immediate need to have all types of personnel for their different units, seeking to make the system operational. It should be as austere as possible without delaying the management of the company's plans and programs.

Among its characteristics, it must:

1. Go adjusted according to the needs of the company.

2. Be elastic.

3. To be governed by its nature.

- **Financial Budget**

It consists of fixing the estimates of sales investment, miscellaneous income to finally elaborate a cash flow that measures the economic and real state of the company. Understand:

- Revenue budget (the gross total without deducting expenses).

- Budget of expenditures (to determine the liquid or net).

- Net flow (difference between income and expenses).

- Final box.

- Initial box.

- Minimum box.

- **Treasury Budget**

It is formulated with the expected estimation of funds available in cash, banks and securities of easy realization. It is also known as cash or cash budget because it consolidates all transactions related to the inflow of monetary funds, such as cash sales, portfolio recoveries, financial income, etc., or to the outflow of liquid funds caused by the freezing of debts or amortization of credits or suppliers or payment of payroll, taxes or dividends. It is formulated or presented in two short periods: months or quarters. It can be said that the cash budget is based on the control of estimated to be spent.

- **Capitalizable Investment Budget**

This type of budget seeks to control all investments in fixed assets such as the acquisition of land, construction, expansion or remodeling of buildings, and purchase of machinery and equipment, serving to evaluate possible investment alternatives and know the amount of funds required and their availability in time with which you can know at what time the information will be required to determine when to take the most viable alternatives for the development of the plan.

123

• Public Budget

They are those that governments, states, decentralized companies, etc., elaborate to control the finances of their different dependencies. These quantify the resources required for normal operation, investment and servicing of the public debt of official agencies and entities.

Within the public budget is contemplated:

Public revenues and their classification: Public capital resources or income are all forms of grouping, ordering and presenting public resources, in order to make analyses and projections of the economic and financial type required in a given period. Its classification depends on the type of analysis or study that is desired to carry out, however, generally three classifications are used that are:

1. According to their periodicity

This groups income according to the frequency with which the tax authorities receive it. They can be classified as ordinary and extraordinary. The ordinary ones are those that are collected periodically and permanently from traditional sources, made up of taxes, fees and other periodic means of financing by the State. The income, extraordinary by exclusion, would be those that do not meet these requirements.

2. Economic

Government revenue is classified or broken down into flows, capital resources and financial sources.

Current income is income from tax, non-tax and transfers received to finance current expenses. Capital resources are those arising from the sale of fixed assets, furniture and real estate, compensation for losses or damage to property, collection of loans granted, reduction of inventories, etc.

Financial sources are generated by the decrease in financial assets (use of availabilities, sale of bonds and shares, recovery of loans, etc.) and the increase in liabilities (obtaining loans, increase in accounts payable, etc.).

3. By sector of orgigin

This classification is based on one of the aspects that characterize the economic structure of Venezuela, where a high proportion of products are made in oil and iron activities, which implies that most of the income comes from operations carried out abroad. This classification presents the following:

1. External Sector
    o Oil Tankers
    o Income from iron
    o Exchange rate gain

- o External indebtedness
2. Internal Sector
    - o Taxes
    - o Fees
    - o Territorial Domain
    - o Internal Indebtedness
    - o Other Income

Public expenditure and its classification

These budgets contemplate the different ways of presenting the public expenditures foreseen in the budget, with the purpose of analyzing them, providing also information for the general study of the economy and the economic policy that the National Government intends to apply for a determined period. The different ways of classifying public expenditure in the public budget are presented below:

- **Institutional Classification**

It orders the public expenditures of the institutions or dependencies to which budgetary appropriations are allocated, in a given period, for the fulfillment of their objectives.

- **Classification by nature of expenditure**

It allows to identify the goods and services that are acquired with the allocations foreseen in the budget and the destination of the transfers, by means of a systematic and homogeneous order of these and of the transfers, and of the variations of assets and liabilities that the public sector applies in the development of its productive process.

- **Economic Classification**

It arranges public expenditures according to the basic structure of the system of national accounts in order to link the results of public transactions with the system, and also allows for the analysis of the effects of public activity on the national economy.

Description of the main headings of the economic classification:

A. **Current expenses**: consumption or production expenses, such as property income and transactions granted to other components of the economic system to finance such expenses.

B. **Capital expenditures**: are expenditures for real investment and capital transfers made for that purpose to exponents of the economic system.

- **Sectoral Classification**

This presents public expenditure disaggregated by economic and social sectors, where it has its effect. It aims to facilitate coordination between development plans and the government budget.

- **Sorting by Program**

This presents public expenditure disaggregated by economic and social sectors, where it has its effect. It seeks to facilitate coordination between development plans and the government budget, the programmed Budget is an instrument that fulfils the purpose of combining available resources in the immediate future, with short-term goals, created for the execution of long-term and medium-term objectives.

- **Regional Classification**

Allows you to sort the expenditure according to the regional destination it is given. It reflects the meaning and scope of the actions carried out by the public sector at the regional level.

- **Budget by Performance**

This budget contains information on how budgeting works to redirect the federal budget process from its focus on inputs to one that also includes the output obtained from the use of such inputs.

- **Mixed Classification**

These are combinations of public expenditures, which are prepared for analysis and decision-making purposes. This type of classification manages to present a series of aspects of great interest, which facilitate the systematic study of public expenditure and the determination of the Budgetary Policy for a given period. The following are the most commonly used mixed classifications:

A. Institutional by program.

B. Institutional by the nature of the expenditure.

C. Economic institutional.

D. Institutional sectorial.

E. By object of economic expenditure.

F. Economic sector.

G. By program and by nature of expenditure.

Private budgets

These are the budgets that individual companies use as an instrument of their administration. They contain the same economic and financial elements in general terms of public sector budgets with some variants in the design of budget allocation items or accounts.

- **Quotation for your content**

These are composed of two types:

Main: This type of budget is a summary, in which the core elements are presented in all the company's budgets.

Auxiliaries: this budget presents in an analytical way all the operations estimated by each one of the departments in charge of the organization of the company.

- **Budgets for your valuation technique**

Dear Ones: These budgets are formulated on an empirical basis. Their numerical figures, because they are determined from previous experiences, represent only the more or less reasonable probability that what has been planned will actually happen.

Standard: this type of budget eliminates the probability of error in a very high percentage, so its figures, unlike the previous ones, represent the results that must be obtained.

- **Budgets based on their reflection in the financial statements**

Commitment item: This type of budget shows the static position that the company would have in the future, if the predictions were fulfilled. It is presented by means of what is known as a budgeted commitment item (balance sheet).

Of results: they show the possible profits to obtain in a future period.

Of costs: they are prepared taking as base the principles established in the sales forecasts, and they reflect, to a future period, the disbursements that have to be made for the total cost or any of its parts.

- **Budgets based on their purpose**

By promotion: they are presented in the form of a financial and expansion project; for their elaboration it is necessary to estimate the income and expenses that have to be carried out in the budgetary period.

By application: these are normally prepared for credit applications. They constitute general forecasts on the distribution of the resources that the company has or will have to have.

By merger: they are used to determine in advance the operations that will result from a conjunction of entities.

By areas and levels of responsibility: When you want to quantify the responsibility of those in charge of the areas and levels into which a company is divided.

By programmes: this type of budget is usually created by government agencies, decentralized agencies, trusts, institutions, etc. Its figures express expenditure, in relation to the objectives pursued, determining the cost of the specific activities that each unit must carry out in order to carry out the programmes for which it is responsible.

- **Below Zero Budgets**

This budget is made without taking into consideration the experiences. This budget is useful in view of the excessive and continuous rise in prices, demands for updating, change, and continuous increase in costs at all levels, basically. It is very expensive and with extemporaneous information. The process of analyzing each budget item, starting with the current level of each, and then justifying the additional disbursements that the programmes may require in the next fiscal year, is typical of a public administration and should not be the procedure for deciding in the private sphere.

Cost and its types

We have already discussed in a broad and detailed way some topics that are part of the budgets, but we must also define what is the cost and its types.

The cost is the patrimonial or monetary value of the products or consumption of factors that promote the execution of an economic activity destined to the production of a good, product, service or activity. The cost must be considered in each and every one of the activities that are carried out in life, because in some way it is the price that will be paid to obtain or acquire something.

Costs have different classifications and types:

- **According to their nature**

A. Raw materials and other supplies.

B. External services.

C. Direct and/or indirect labor.

D. Amortization, which is the cost of employing fixed assets in production.

E. Financial, derived from the use of external financial resources.

F. Opportunity costs, which are those costs incurred for not having attended to an available

133

alternative investment or also the value of the best unrealized option.

G. Indirect manufacturing and delivery costs.

- **Explicit and implicit costs**

Since, in the economic area, in addition to monetary transactions, we also study how individuals make their decisions, a distinction is made between implicit and explicit costs:

a) **Explicit cost** is that which can be expressed in monetary terms; that is, it requires the use of money for its payment.

b) **Implicit cost** is that which cannot be expressed in monetary terms; that is, as an opportunity cost.

- **According to the application of the factors to the products**

Depending on the application of the factors to the products being manufactured, a distinction is made between direct costs and indirect costs.

a) **Direct costs:** they are characterized by their calculation that can be assigned in a certain way to a product. For example, in the manufacture of a newspaper, the cost of paper consumed is a direct cost, because the exact amount of paper needed to make a newspaper can be known, while the cost of cleaning the manufacturing hall is an indirect cost in the production of a good.

b) **Indirect costs**: these are affected globally and since they cannot be directly assigned to a product, they must be previously distributed through the so-called primary cost sharing table.

- **Fixed and variable costs**

These are established depending on the fluctuation of the currency with which they are studied and establish the budgets:

Variable cost, which includes those costs that vary at the same rate as production, such as the cost derived from the consumption of water in a soft drink factory, this cost is clearly variable. It is important to point out that the definition of variable corresponds to total cost, because as the element that makes its value vary in its totality changes, it will cause the value or cost to vary or fluctuate proportionally; however, in unitary terms, in a scenario of a perfect economy and constant prices, a cost that appears as a variable on a total scale has a fixed behavior on a unitary scale. For example, if a person buys a ticket to go to an event, the total cost will correspond to a person multiplied by the cost price of admission to the event, if people are added, the total cost of attending the event will vary proportionally, however, when calculating the unit cost, i.e. the total cost divided by attendees, it will have a directly fixed behavior.

Examples of variable costs:

- The fuel consumption used in a vehicle.

- Sales commissions paid to a seller.

- The rent of a dependency in a shopping center that has a payment based on the sales it makes.

- All the examples mentioned above have in common that "there is something that makes them vary", in the case of fuel consumption varies depending on the kilometers traveled, depreciation depending on the hours spent, commissions based on sales made as well as the rental of the unit in the mall.

Fixed cost is adapted by companies independently to the quantity produced, so the cost does not increase when the quantity produced increases, nor does it decrease when the quantity produced does, and even in an extreme case must be borne even when the quantity produced is nil. In reality, costs only behave like fixed costs in the short term, because in the long term they all have a variable character. Thus, the cost of renting a premise contracted for one year, will be a fixed cost during that annual time that must be paid regardless of the amount manufactured or sold of a good.

Examples of fixed costs:

- The depreciation of a vehicle calculated on the basis of years of useful life.

- Monthly Fire Insurance Fee

- The basic salary of a seller of products.

- Renting a shopping center without variable components.

In all the examples above, the cost remains regardless of whether there is or is a level of activity, i.e. if the company closes for vacation, it must still assume these costs.

- **Standard Cost**

A budgeted value or cost that is based on normal efficiency levels. It is developed based on the budgeted direct and indirect values or costs. It is a measure of how much it should cost to produce a unit of product or service always under conditions of efficiency, i.e. no waste, idle time, etc. This cost is composed of the costs of the components required to make a product.

An example of this cost may be a leather jacket, which includes:

1. Cost of Direct Materials (leather, zipper, buttons, etc.).

2. Direct Labor Cost (the time required to cut the design, sew it, etc. multiplied by the production rate of the employees influencing the process).

3. Indirect or manufacturing costs related to the product (depreciation of the leather cutting machine, electricity, factory rent, etc.).

Elements making up the cost of production

There are many elements that must be taken into account when contemplating the cost within a budget, and they are composed by:

- **The materials.** These are the main resources used in production. These are transformed into finished goods with the help of labor and indirect manufacturing costs. They are conformed by:

  a) **Direct.** All those costs that can be identified in the manufacture of a finished product, easily related to it and represent the main cost of materials in the manufacture of a product.

  b) **Indirect.** They are those who are involved in the elaboration of a product, but they have a relative relevance in front of the direct ones.

  c) **Manpower.** It is the physical or mental effort used for the elaboration of a product.

- **Manpower.** It is the physical or mental effort used for the elaboration of a product.

  a) **Straight up.** It is the labor directly involved in the manufacture of a finished product that can be easily associated with it and that has great cost in processing.

b) **Indirect.** It is labor that does not have a significant cost at the time of production of the product.

- Indirect manufacturing costs (CIF). They are all those costs that accumulate from materials and indirect labor plus all those incurred in production but that at the time of obtaining the cost of the finished product are not easily identifiable directly with it.

Do you know what the ABC (Activity Based Costing) model is?

It is a model that allows the allocation and distribution of the different indirect costs, according to the activities carried out, since these are the ones that really generate costs. This system arises from the need to provide a solution to the problems normally associated with standard costs when they do not faithfully reflect the value-added chain in the production of a given product or service and, therefore, an adequate determination of the price is not possible.

The ABC cost model allocates and distributes indirect costs according to the activities carried out in the process of making the product or service, identifying the origin of the cost with the necessary activity, not only for production but also for distribution and sale. This activity is understood as the set of actions aimed at adding value to the product through the manufacturing process. The ABC Model is based on the fact that products and services consume activities, which in turn generate costs.

Phases for Implementing the ABC Cost Model

The phases of the ABC cost model are broken down below:

Activities: homologating products, negotiating prices, classifying suppliers, disappointing materials, planning production, issuing orders, invoicing, charging, designing new products, etc.

Processes: purchasing, sales, finance, personnel, planning, research and development, etc.

The activities and processes to be operational from the point of view of efficiency, need to be homogeneous to measure them in operational functions of the products.

Stages for cost allocation

- **First stage:** costs are classified into a group of general costs or pool for which variations can be explained by a single cost-driver.

- **Second step:** In this step, the unit cost of each pool is assigned to the products. This is done using the pool key figure calculated in the first step and the measure of the amount of resources consumed by each product.

How much does a budget influence savings?

Let's talk again about the budget, now geared towards personal or family savings. The budget has a positive effect because you learn and start controlling your expenses and savings.

To create your monthly budget, you must keep in mind that you must know exactly how much you spend per month, and then compare that amount with the liquid income received. If the expense that has been estimated is maintained and respected, it will be possible to determine in which areas it is possible to reduce expenses and if it is finally spent less than the income that is obtained, there will be the money to save.

How to calculate?

To determine a person's ability to pay, which is the maximum amount for which they can borrow, you must do the following:

- You start by determining your net monthly income (liquid compensation).

- From that you subtract the sum of fixed costs that you have each month. In other words, the payments for food, rent or dividends, school fees, basic services (electricity, water, gas, telephone, cable and others) are subtracted.

- Other expenses must be added such as benzine, clothes and footwear, fun, a monthly expense must be estimated.

- If debt payments exist, they must also be subtracted.

If the final result is zero or close to zero, it means that the person will not be able to save and should not take credit either, as he or she will not be able to pay for it.

Conversely, if it is possible for you to reduce monthly payments and eventually spend less than the income you earn, there will be money to save.

Finally, the monthly budget helps identify what each month's money is used on and monitor its use.

Another great strategy for budget management is the 50/20/30 rule.

This strategy consists of 50% for your most basic expenses, 20% for savings and 30% for your personal expenses. In this way you will be able to know your expenses at all times, and thus know how much money you dedicate to saving. How does it work?

1. 50% of your paycheck money is for basic expenses. These go on the mortgage, bills, community, shopping basket of the month, etc. These are expenses that you must carry out yes or yes. That's why they cover 50% of your salary, to prevent. If you have money left over, so much the better. Don't spend it on unnecessary things and add it to the next percentage.

2. 20% of the money you earn has to go into saving. This money is going to be a mattress that will save you against possible future debts, reforms in your house or changes in your family. And if you're young, it's the best time to save, because when you're older you'll appreciate having saved a good money from this method.

3. The last 30% goes to personal expenses. I mean, anything you can do during the month. Maybe you buy some clothes, another month you can spend on more leisure activities, travel or you may have a few birthdays. That's where you have

to spend this 30%. And I remind you, if it's too much, add it to the 20% savings.

Important tips for developing a functional budget

You know the importance of establishing a correct budget, adjusted to the goals and objectives set, so here are some useful tips to develop a potential budget, which has no losses or waste:

- **Analyze your needs and desires**. Evaluate your current economic situation and environment. Make a list of needs and a list of wants by answering these questions:

1. Why do I want this?

2. What would I change in my life if I had it? (for better or worse)

3. What are the really important things for me?

4. What do I need to live in happiness and comfort?

- **Make a list of your priorities.** The budget is based on needs and desires but spending priorities must be established. Some of them are:

1. Housing

2. Food & Beverage

3. Mobilization

4. Clothing

5. Health

6. Education

7. Savings

- **Define smart goals**. Make sure your goals are:

  a) **Specific**: Know exactly what you will spend your money on. For example: make a trip (don't save by saving).

  b) **Measurable:** Know what your goal is. It has to be a set number.

  c) **Achievable:** Possible steps. Example: knowing that you can cut expenses to save enough each month to pay for it.

  d) **Relevant:** Relate to your needs and desires. Example: staying in luxury hotels during the trip.

  e) **Defined time:** Concrete date to reach the goal. Example: travel in December.

- **Add up your income.** Includes all sources of income: salaries, interest, investments, pensions, etc.

- **Add up your expenses.** The best way to do this is to write down every penny you spend every day for at least a month.

- **Calculate the difference.** With this operation you will know the difference between what you earn, spend and have available (or not) to reach a goal, access a credit, have an emergency fund, etc.

1. Identify fixed costs first

If you don't have a family budget, the beginning of the year is a good time to start putting your finances in order. Remember that all recommendations can be summed up in one: don't spend more than you earn. And for this it is essential to know how much he earns and how much he spends. To calculate your expenses, you must first identify which ones are fixed and how much they add up per month.

2. Variable expenses

The second part of preparing a budget is to identify your variable expenses: for example, trips to the movies or meals away from home, among others. An important variable expense, more for the difficulty of its control than for its amount, is the denominated "ant expense", that is to say, those small payments that a person makes throughout the day and that finally constitute a greater amount.

3. Distribution in the couple

A good option is for everyone to assume 50% of the fixed costs. Another formula that works is that fixed costs are apportioned in proportion to the amount of each spouse's income. And a third alternative is that one of them, either the man or the woman, takes over 100% and the other takes care of the work at home.

4. Revenues are also ordered

The part of the expense is the most difficult to sort. But income also needs to be observed.

5. Spend less than you save

Savings should not be what over income, the ideal is to establish a certain amount for savings, whether to have an emergency fund or for some travel or initial share of a durable good, in addition, the budget should be organized in such a way that expenses are less than income.

6. Periodic review of the budget

Once you have assembled your budget, you must update it every month.

Final recommendations that positively influence budgets

Many financial experts say that in order for your monthly income to last, you must do the following:

1. **Pay your monthly bills.** There are many penalties if you pay your bills late, such as late fees, losing possession of things you've bought on credit, and even being evicted from an apartment.

2. **Set aside the money you will need** for your weekly and daily expenses, such as food and bus fare.

3. **Put money into savings**. Try to accumulate two months of net salary to use in case of an unexpected financial emergency.

4. **Set aside money for large expenses** you know will occur, such as car repairs or appliance repairs.

5. **Set aside money for your big future goals, whether it's** a home, college education for your children, a new car or a trip.

6. **Try to spread the bills evenly throughout the month**, so that you pay about the same amount each week. For regular monthly accounts, you may be able to ask for a change in the due date to better distribute your accounts. Try to avoid weeks when all of your available money is needed to pay bills.

7. **For large expenses that are not monthly**, for example: insurance bills, car repairs, holiday gifts, etc. Keep an amount of money each week or pay

period so you have money to pay bills when they are due.

8. Seek **guidance** in considering how much of your net monthly income you could budget for various expenses:

- Housing as rent or mortgage, from 20 to 35%.

- Basic services such as gas, electricity, water, garbage collection, telephone from 4 to 7%.

- Lunch at home and away from home, from 15 to 30%.

- Family needs such as laundry, toiletries, hair care, 2-4%.

- Medical expenses such as insurance, medications, bills, 2 to 8%.

- Clothes 3 to 10%.

- Transportation such as car payment, gasoline, insurance, repairs or bus cost, 6 to 30%.

- Entertainment from 2 to 6%.

- Savings of 10 to 15%.

9. Try to limit your debts in installments (car loans, credit card accounts, other loans) to 10-20% of your monthly budget.

10. To decide if an expense is necessary, ask yourself the following questions:

- Do I really need it?

- Do I really need it today? What if I didn't buy it now?

- Can I meet this need at a lower expense?

11. Always review your bank and credit card statements. They'll remind you where your money goes.

Conclusion

Did you notice how important it is to establish a correct budget?

Everything in life consists of planning, as this maintains order and discipline in any society. Nowadays there are several methods that can allow you to put your life in order, from hiring a simple personal assistant to downloading an application on your cell phone that can take you the management of your finances based on your income and expenses, so that you do not abuse or waste more money than you can recover. The success of any businessman is that he has the financial intelligence to establish budgets, plans and execute work plans with a capital or investment meticulously programmed and destined for each activity, that, executed in a correct way, will give the return of that investment plus a profit that can be little or enough, depending on the impact that product had in the market.

In the book we also emphasize the great importance of the cost factor of the products or goods that must be contemplated in the budgets. While it is true that the best quality has a higher cost, sometimes we see cases in which they abuse that feature, so you should always look for various options so you can study the market and know what may be the best option in price, value and quality of the product, and do not go with the first thing you get, so whether it is a 5% or 10% that you can save on each expense, is a percentage and money that you will accumulate and, in a long term can be reflected into important savings for you.

A good option can be to buy products wholesale, in large quantities, which, although it can be a hard blow for the moment, can mean a saving of up to 40% or 50% of savings, and you can even sell with a profit margin in your favor to someone you know or family to recover and improve that investment. Many people use this strategy, because it always works, but be careful, the fact that you buy in large quantities does not mean that you will spend in large quantities.

Now, if you are a manager in a company, or you depend on important financial decisions in a company or organization, you must be very careful, because there the costs are much higher, and budgets include a greater number of elements to take into account for the formation of a budget line. Each time you need to make a budget, detail each of the items or elements that make up that budget, assess whether its quality is the most optimal, is the most appropriate to cover the need that the organization has at that time, because if the price is proportional to the quality of the product, if the quantities are not exaggerated but you are budgeting the right amount, and above all, the life time that will provide the final product after approving the budget, i.e. how long the product that the company will acquire when the budget is approved.

If you are the head of the family, put together a list of basic expenses per month, for example, how much you spend monthly on food (without exaggerating with unnecessary luxuries such as sweets, alcohol, etc.), on paying for services such as electricity, water, rent (if applicable), condominium, internet, telephone or cable television, in addition to other necessary expenses such as paying for the transportation of family members (children or couple), children's tuition, school fees, among other expenses. Try not to get out of those monthly costs or expenses, that is, to surpass them, on the contrary, try to reduce or maintain them each month, and, consequently, you must try to earn monthly that amount of money with a surplus of 20% above that budget so you can count on savings capacity. Remember that this saving will be your life mattress at some less expected time. If you have a partner, try to share the expenses, and build a fund between the two for the family, save for some family vacations in the future, remodeling the house, or more importantly, build a college fund for your children or future children, and even a retirement fund for when they have completed the quota of working life, that is to say, when each one turns more than 65 and they must retire for that moment, although the best option for this is to invest in a venture or company that can give dividends in a passive way without you as owner having to work it regularly, but on the contrary, just monitor that everything works in order.

CPSIA information can be obtained
at www.ICGtesting.com
Printed in the USA
BVHW030912101022
649064BV00018B/577

9 781647 773243